D0048082

Personal Oracle RAC Clusters
Create Oracle 10g Grid Computing at Home

Edward Stoever

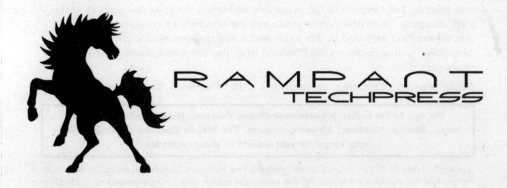

SHROFF PUBLISHERS & DISTRIBUTORS PVT. LTD.
Mumbai   Bangalore   Chennai   Kolkata   New Delhi

Personal Oracle RAC Clusters
Create Oracle 10g Grid Computing at Home

By Edward Stoever

Copyright © 2006 by Rampant TechPress. All rights reserved. ISBN: 0-9761573-8-1

Originally Printed in the United States of America.

Published by Rampant TechPress, Kittrell, North Carolina, USA.

Library of Congress Control Number: 2005928149

Easy Oracle Series: Book #7

Editors: John Lavender, Janet Burleson, and Linda Webb

Production Editor: Teri Wade

Production Manager: Linda Webb

Cover Design: Steve Karam

Illustrations: Mike Reed

Printing History:

June 2006 for First Edition

First Indian Reprint: July 2007

ISBN - 10: 81-8404-345-7

ISBN - 13: 978-81-8404-345-7

Published by **Shroff Publishers and Distributors Pvt. Ltd.** C-103, MIDC, TTC Industrial Area, Pawane, Navi Mumbai 400 701, Tel: (91 22) 2763 4290, Fax: (91 22) 2768 3337, e-mail: spdorders@shroffpublishers.com. Printed at Decora Printers, Mumbai.

I dedicate this book to my two daughters, Scarlett and Veronica.
- *Daddy loves you!*

Table of Contents

Using the Online Code Depot

Purchase of this book provides complete access to the online code depot that contains the sample code scripts. All of the code depot scripts in this book are located at the following URL:

http://www.rampant.cc/personal-rac.htm

All of the code scripts in this book are available for download in zip format, ready to load and use. If technical assistance is needed with downloading or accessing the scripts, please contact Rampant TechPress at info@rampant.cc.

Are you WISE?

Get the premier Oracle tuning tool. The Workload Interface Statistical Engine for Oracle provides unparallel capability for time-series Oracle tuning, unavailable nowhere else.

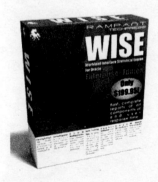

WISE supplements Oracle Enterprise Manager and it can quickly plot and spot performance signatures to allow you to see hidden trends, fast.

WISE interfaces with STATSPACK or AWR to provide unprecedented proactive tuning insights. Best of all, it is only $9.95. Get WISE download Now!

www.wise-oracle.com

Got Scripts?

This is the complete Oracle script collection from Mike Ault and Donald Burleson, the world's best Oracle DBA's.

Packed with over 600 ready-to-use Oracle scripts, this is the definitive collection for every Oracle professional DBA. It would take many years to develop these scripts from scratch, making this download the best value in the Oracle industry.

It's only $49.95 (less than 7 cents per script!). For immediate download go to:

www.oracle-script.com

Conventions Used in this Book

It is critical for any technical publication to follow rigorous standards and employ consistent punctuation conventions to make the text easy to read.

However, this is not an easy task. Within Oracle there are many types of notation that can confuse a reader. Some Oracle utilities such as STATSPACK and TKPROF are always spelled in CAPITAL letters, while Oracle parameters and procedures have varying naming conventions in the Oracle documentation. It is also important to remember that many Oracle commands are case sensitive, and are always left in their original executable form, and never altered with italics or capitalization.

Hence, all Rampant TechPress books follow these conventions:

Parameters - All Oracle parameters will be lowercase italics. Exceptions to this rule are parameter arguments that are commonly capitalized (KEEP pool, TKPROF), these will be left in ALL CAPS.

Variables - All PL/SQL program variables and arguments will also remain in *lowercase italics* (*dbms_job, dbms_utility*).

Tables & dictionary objects – All data dictionary objects are referenced in *lowercase italics* (*dba_indexes, v$sql*). This includes all *v$* and *x$* views (*x$kcbcbh, v$parameter*) and dictionary views (*dba_tables, user_indexes*).

SQL - All SQL is formatted for easy use in the code depot. The main SQL terms (select, from, where, group by, order by, having) will always appear on a separate line.

Programs & Products - All products and programs that are known to the author are capitalized according to the vendor specifications (IBM, DBXray, etc). All names known by Rampant TechPress to be trademark names appear in this text as initial caps. References to UNIX are always made in uppercase.

Acknowledgements

Acknowledgements

A lot of behind-the-scenes effort went into writing and producing this book. The following people and institutions have had a profound effect on my career, knowledge, skills and ambition.

Vladimir Lugo, a wonderful friend and mentor. My zeal for Oracle software comes in great part from Vladimir. Had it not been for Vladimir's enthusiasm for Oracle RAC technology, this book would not have been written.

Juan Rodriguez and the staff at Integrated Digital Technologies. IDT is a great place to teach and learn about software and computer technology. Thank you for providing me so many opportunities.

Bill Roberts, my supervisor and friend at Fuller Seminary. One of my greatest blessings has been Bill's support and encouragement.
Fuller Theological Seminary, Pasadena, CA., my full time employer. Fuller has been and continues to be the best place to work that I have ever experienced. Fuller is supportive, compassionate and family oriented. Special thanks to my co-workers in the MIS department.

Jeff Harwell, dedicated technical editor, Linux authority and friend. I cannot find the words to express my thanks for your work on this book!

Don Burleson and the Staff at Rampant Tech Press. This book was an amazing opportunity for me. You have stood behind me throughout the process and I am most grateful.

My sincerest thanks to all,

Edward Stoever
Database Administrator
Fuller Theological Seminary
Pasadena, California

6   Preface

Preface

As an Oracle Database Administrator or as a student studying to be an Oracle DBA, you certainly know the job at hand requires constant training. To have a successful career as an Oracle DBA, you must strive to learn new things always.

This book covers a very hot topic for DBAs: building Real Application Cluster (RAC) databases. We have all heard the hype. We have all seen and read books and articles on the subject. RAC technology is a cornerstone to Oracle's grid technology. But have you ever built a RAC database?

When it comes to Oracle software, most people will not understand the complicated concepts until they have learned by doing. This is your opportunity to do something that many DBAs only talk about. With the help of this book, you will build a Real Application Cluster with three different releases of Oracle Software, upgrading databases as you go.

There are many things that could prevent you from building a RAC database. It certainly takes time and money. The licensing fee for an operating system that Oracle is certified to run on is enough a barrier to make most people stop right there. This book breaks through that barrier by building a RAC database on a completely free version of Linux. In fact, all the software used in this book is freely downloadable on the internet as of the date of publication - and if things change, you can visit the support website for alternatives.

Keeping costs to a minimum is critical, especially for students. The exercise in this book uses low-priced personal computers and inexpensive external storage. About half of the items I used to put my system together were given to me by friends and

---

family. Even if you have to purchase all the required hardware, this project can be done for less than one thousand dollars, a small price to pay for the experience you will gain.

If you do not know much about Linux, do not be discouraged. This book takes into account that many DBAs and students have never used Linux and is written with that in mind.

One thing that you will learn from this exercise is that Oracle software is not perfect by any means. It can be buggy and error prone, especially when installed on non-certified hardware and on a non-certified operating system. I have put great care into documenting my experiences for your aid. Nevertheless, I am expecting you to run into trouble at least a few times. Appendix C will provide the solutions I have found for the typical errors that may arise. In Oracle's defense, I must admit most of the errors I experienced were caused by my own misunderstandings or mistakes.

Another valuable resource available with use of this book is the support website at http://www..rampant.cc/personal-rac.htm There, you will find updates, errata, a FAQ, articles and information. You will also have the opportunity to participate by asking questions. I look forward to meeting you online.

Edward Stoever
Oracle Database Administrator
Fuller Theological Seminary, Pasadena California

Acquiring the Required Hardware

Objective

The goal of this book is to assemble a functioning Oracle Real Application Cluster database on hardware that can be purchased easily and inexpensively.

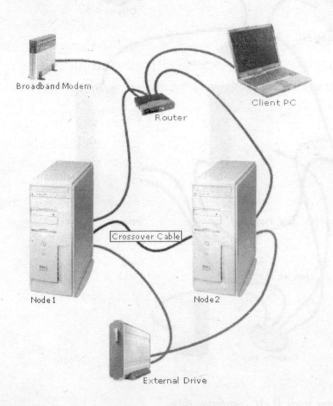

Figure 1.1: *Two node RAC configuration.*

Figure 1.1 shows the hardware configuration of a two node RAC. Each node has two network interface cards and one firewire card. The crossover cable is an internal network that supports Oracle's cache fusion. This internal network allows the nodes to communicate very quickly, which is necessary to keep the buffer cache of each node in synch with the buffer cache of the other.

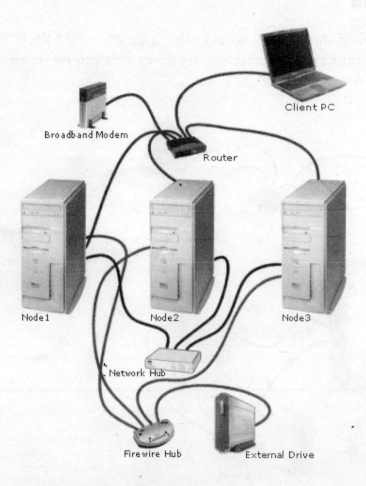

Figure 1.2: *Three node RAC configuration.*

If a third node is needed, a network hub for the internal network and a firewire hub for the external disk drive will be required as shown in Figure 1.2. Notice that the cross-over cable is replaced by standard network cables.

The following table examines the items needed to build a two node Oracle RAC, and includes estimates for what it will cost to purchase each item:

ITEM	ESTIMATED COST	AUTHOR'S NOTES
Two nodes	$400.00 for both.	The nodes should be Pentium 3's or higher. For this book, two used Dell Dimension 4100 Computers were purchased on ebay.com for $200 each. Each computer included one hard drive with a capacity of 10 to 20 gigabytes and at least 256 Megabytes of ram.
Four Network Interface Cards	$20 to $50 for all four.	Refurbished NIC cards are generally available at Fry's electronics for $5 each.
Two 1394 Firewire cards	$40 to $70 for both.	The firewire cards were purchased for $20 each at CompUSA.
One Crossover Cable - 3ft.	$5	If a crossover cable cannot be found, a hub and two standard network cables will work in its place.
Two Network Cables - 15ft	$15	
One Extra Firewire Cable	$10	
Additional CD Roms	$50	Each node will require a CD Rom device; one with the ability to burn CDs.
Additional RAM	$100	Each node will require no less than 512 megabytes of RAM. A 9i RAC database can be built with less RAM installed in each node, but creating 10g databases with less than 512 megabytes will most likely fail.
One Monitor	$0 to $100	A 15 inch monitor will work just fine, though a 17 inch monitor is ideal.
One Keyboard and Mouse	$0 to $30	

ITEM	ESTIMATED COST	AUTHOR'S NOTES
One 2-port KVM switch.	$50	A Belkin model with built in cabling was purchased. To switch between the two nodes, the user types {scroll lock} {scroll lock} {up-arrow}.
One wired network router	$30	
One power strip	$5	
One External Hard Drive	$225	The Maxtor model A01A200 was used for this book. This hard disk allows for dual logging which is required. LaCie also makes external drives that work. When in doubt, get the Maxtor model. Do not buy any brand of hard disk just because it is firewire. Most likely it will not allow for dual logging and will fail.
Two additional internal hard drives	$50 for both	Appendix C of this book covers how to take an image copy of the operating system to be able to restore to a previous point. The ideal method is to use an extra hard disk of 3 to 10 gigabytes in each node.
One Client Computer with networking support.	$0	It is assumed that an additional windows computer is available. This is required to burn CDs and will be used as a client of the database.
Broadband internet service	$30 per month	
Blank CDs	$10	At least 10 blank CDs are required.
One Card table, 2' x 4'	$30	

Table 1.1: *Items needed to build a two node Oracle RAC*

Before purchasing anything, it is a good idea to ask family, friends and neighbors for computer parts that are no longer in use. Many of the items in this list can be found collecting dust in someone's garage or basement. Most people are more than happy to get rid of such "junk."

Try to obtain two internal hard drives for each node. The first hard drive of a given node will need a capacity of at least 10 gigabytes. It will be used to store the operating system and the Oracle software. The second hard drive for a node should have a capacity of three or more gigabytes. It will be used to store a compressed image of the first drive. An image of the primary hard drive will allow you to quickly revert to a pervious point in the project, without having to reinstall and reconfigure from the very beginning.

Below are a few tips for assembling the hardware:

- Put all the hardware together *before* installing the operating systems or software.

- If working with used computers, purchase a can of compressed air to safely blow away the accumulated dust.

- When putting the hardware together, avoid working in a room with carpeting. Carpeting generates static electricity and static electricity can ruin electronics. If this cannot be avoided, keep yourself grounded with a grounding strap as you assemble the hardware. Never place a network card, firewire card, RAM board or other unprotected electronic devices directly on a carpeted surface.

- When a NIC card or other device is pushed into a slot on the motherboard so that it seats properly (resting flush at the bottom of the slot), sometimes the bracket will not align with the screw-hole on the case. Do not force the card out of its alignment to make the bracket conform to the screw-hole. It is better to take the card out, bend the bracket to fit and then reinsert the card.

- Install the internal hard disks so that they share one IDE cable. Doing so will make it possible for the CD ROM drive to be on a separate cable. If the CD ROM must be on the same cable as a hard disk, ensure that the hard disk is the master and that the CD ROM is the slave.

- When two devices share the same IDE cable, one device must be set as the master and one must be set as the slave. There are two methods for doing this. The first method is to indicate directly which device is which with the appropriate jumper settings. The second is the cable select method. To use the cable select method, set the jumpers on both devices to the cable select setting. The device at the final end of the cable will be the master and the other will be the slave.

- Many hard drives have a diagram on the outside showing the jumper settings for master, slave, and cable select. Some older drives do not. To find the jumper settings for any drive, use a search engine to search for the drive model number and the words "jumper master slave."

- Remove any unnecessary cards that may be plugged into the mother board such as sound cards or SCSI cards.

- Once all of the internal hardware is connected, turn on the computer and enter the BIOS setup. Common methods for entering setup are pressing the delete key, the F1 key or the F2 key before the system boots from disk. Upon entering setup, double check that the system detects the internal hard disks, the RAM, the CD ROM and the floppy drive if applicable. Verify that the system boots from the CD ROM before it boots from the hard disk.

- When the internal hardware is completely installed and the covers of the nodes are closed, connect the firewire drive to the firewire ports of each node and then turn the drive on on.

Conclusion

With the two nodes completely put together and the external cables attached, as shown in Figure 1.1, you are now ready to proceed to installing the Linux operating system on each node.

Installing Linux

This chapter will give instructions to overcome common problems when installing Linux for the first time. It will then cover setting up the desktop and network for Oracle RAC use.

Obtaining the Linux Install Disks

This project uses a distribution of Linux called Fedora. As this book goes to print, there are four distributions of Fedora available: Core 1, Core 2, Core 3 and Core 4. Although the most recent version is Core 4, the project in this book requires Core 1. Core 1 is the only release that supports all of the Oracle software packages that will be installed. Check the support website for this book at http://www.database-expert.com/rac to learn if this has changed since the time of publication. The password is nyassa.

The following section describes the process of downloading files to a Microsoft Windows computer and using its CD burner to create the install disks.

To download Fedora Core 1, visit the following web page:

```
http://download.fedora.redhat.com/pub/fedora/linux/core/1/i386/iso/
```

Alternatively, a list of mirror sites can be found on this web page:

```
http://fedora.redhat.com/download/mirrors.html
```

Download the three files with the names *yarrow-i386-disc1.iso*, *yarrow-i386-disc2.iso* and *yarrow-i386-disc3.iso*. The files are over 600 megabytes each, so downloading will require your patience even when using a broadband internet connection.

There is a method available to verify that the downloaded files are uncorrupted. On the Core 1 download page is a link marked "MD5SUM." Click the link to find text that reads in part:

```
76ef22495d186580e47efd8d7a65fe6b  yarrow-i386-disc1.iso
fd23fe32fafe7557f5d1fa1d31100580  yarrow-i386-disc2.iso
6a26b34069639d0c31465d4079a8e1b2  yarrow-i386-disc3.iso
```

The numbers associated with each file are checksums that can be reproduced with a windows tool called MD5SUMMER, by Luke Pascoe. This software is available for download at http://www.md5summer.org. Reproducing the checksums ensures not only that the downloads have completed in their entirety, but also that no corruption has taken place during the download process.

The next step is to use the program, Nero, to burn the images to the CDs. NERO can be downloaded and used for 30 days free of charge by visiting the website at http://www.nero.com and browsing to the downloads page. Nero makes burning an ISO image to a CD very easy. After installing Nero on windows, open the Nero StartSmart Program. Mouseover the Copy and Backup Icon and then click on "Burn Image to disk". Nero will open another program and a dialog in which to open a file as shown in Figure 2.1.

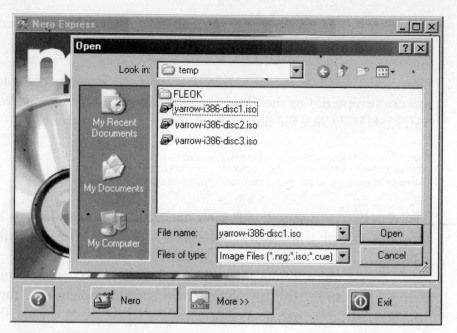

Figure 2.1: *Burning a CD image with Nero Burning ROM.*

At the bottom of the screen, where the label reads "files of type", select "Image Files (*.nrg, *.iso, *.cue)" and browse to the appropriate directory. Select the *yarrow-i386-disc1.iso* file and click "open". Now click "next" to burn it. Repeat this process for the images of disk two and three. Label each disk appropriately so as not to confuse one with the other. Disk one is a bootable disk.

This project requires two more image disks. Visit this website: http://www.sysresccd.org/ and download the stable x86 version of the System Rescue CD. Burn two CDs of that image in the same manner as with the Fedora images. This software will allow you to boot to a Linux operating system on CDROM where recovery operations can be performed if necessary. Also, this software will allow you to take compressed images of your Linux partitions. Be sure to label each CD appropriately.

Installing Fedora Core 1

Installing Fedora Core 1 is simple. There are just a few things you will need to understand as you go through the installation process. To begin, boot the computer to the install disk one. The first screen will look similar to the following:

```
To install or upgrade in graphical mode, press the <ENTER> key.
To install or upgrade in text mode, type: linux text <ENTER>.
Use the function keys listed below for more information.
[F1-Main] [F2-Options] [F3-General] [F4-Kernel] [F5-Rescue]
boot:
```

In most cases simply typing the word "enter" will get the install going without a hitch. But on a few occasions an install can hang at the beginning or encounter an error while trying to detect every hardware item on the system. This is frustrating because rebooting to the CD just causes this to occur again. To get past these problems, hit the F2 key, and a number of options will be presented. The first option is:

```
-. To disable hardware probing, type: linux noprobe <ENTER>.
```

Typing linux noprobe will prevent most any problem that occurs when installing Fedora. By choosing this noprobe option, in a later step, the system will ask if any device drivers need to be loaded, just select DONE.

The next step in the installation process gives an opportunity to check the CD media. This step will determine if each CD is burned properly and will take about five minutes to check each one. If the CDs have been used successfully on a previous occasion, then this step can be skipped.

At this point, the install should jump into a graphical interface. The mouse should move a pointer as expected. The mouse can be used to click "next", or you can type ALT+N to get to the next screen. Most screens in this configuration phase are self-explanatory.

When the screen for "Installation Type" appears, choose "Custom." When the screen for "Disk Partitioning Setup" appears, choose "Automatic." At this point, a screen similar to Figure 2.2 will be presented. One of the drives will be used to store the operating system and Oracle software. It should be between 10,000 and 20,000 MB. The other drive will be used solely to save images of the first drive. Ensure that only the checkbox for the drive in which the software is to be installed is checked.

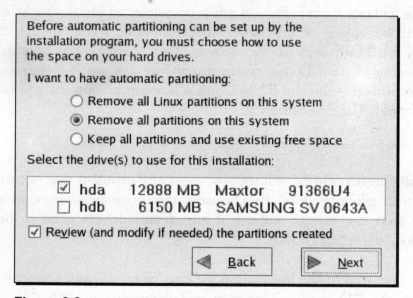

Figure 2.2: *Choosing how Fedora will use the hard drives.*

On the screen for "Network Configuration", two NIC cards should have been detected, and these cards called eth0 and eth1 (this step will be passed over if hardware probing was disabled, which is fine). The boxes for "Active on Boot" can be unchecked, which will save a little time on the node's first boot.

The network will be configured after the install is complete. If the install complains that the computer will not be able to communicate, just click "Continue".

On the screen for "Firewall Configuration", choose "No Firewall." This will cause the install to complain with an alert box, just click "Proceed."

To set the root password, use the same password for all nodes. A password that is easy to remember, but not a dictionary word, is suggested.

On the screen for "Package Group Selection", individual software components can be installed, or at the bottom of the screen, "Everything" can be installed. The author suggests that you select only those items listed in Figure 2.3. Doing so will free up the disk space for Oracle software and save time.

Figure 2.3: *Only these items will be needed for this RAC install.*

The install on the second node can begin as soon as the first node has completed disk 1. When the install is finished on a given node, skip creating an emergency boot disk as this has been done already.

Linux Boots for the First Time

The first time Linux boots, it will go through a few steps. The License Agreement must be accepted; the date and time can be adjusted. It is not necessary to create a user account, even though Fedora may send an alert that this is improper. Finally, the login screen appears and you will login as root.

The desktop area of Fedora is easy to use. There are similarities to Microsoft Windows such as icons on a desktop area and quick launch icons on a bar at the bottom.

One feature not found on windows is the small rectangular area on the toolbar that is divided into four sections. The top left is in dark blue. This box provides access to four different desktop areas. To see it work, click the "globe and mouse" icon. A web browser will open. Now, click a different area of the desktop switcher. A new desktop appears wherein other programs can be used. The previous desktop can still be accessed simply by clicking on the corresponding area of the desktop switcher.

Fedora Linux offers seven login terminals. The seventh is used for the graphical interface. To access each of the seven terminals, type [CTL+ALT+F1] through [CTL+ALT+F7]. This makes it possible to maintain multiple logins simultaneously.

The Linux operating system has an extremely strong set of tools and commands for the command line (see Appendix A for a list of the commands used in this book). It is important to know how to launch a command line terminal from the desktop. Do so by typing [ALT+F1] which will open the Redhat menu. Up arrow to "Run Application" and type [ENTER]. The run-application window appears. Type in gnome-terminal [ENTER]. Gnome-terminal offers some very convenient features such as selecting text with the mouse, copy and paste and color support; just to name a few. It will be from this terminal that you will launch Oracle's Graphical User Interface (GUI) programs such as the Universal Installer.

Initial Setup of the Operating System

Both nodes should have Fedora installed at this time. Use the KVM switch to switch between the two nodes. However, you will quickly realize a problem. It is very difficult to tell which node you are working on because the desktop of one node looks exactly the same as the desktop of the other.

One method to determine which node is on the screen is to insert a CD on one node and not the other. This will place an additional icon on the desktop of the node with the CD inserted. This method is effective but impractical.

A more practical method for determining which node is on the screen is to permanently change the appearance of the desktop environment. Switch to Oracle1, the node on the left. Use the CD trick described above to make sure that Oracle1 is on the screen. Right click the desktop, choose "Change Desktop Background" and a dialog will appear. Click the default image in the top left corner, and the path to that image appears as:

```
/usr/share/backgrounds/images/default.png
```

 Professionally edited desktop and toolbar images, as seen in Figure 2.5, are included in the code depot of this book. If you wish to skip the image editing part of the instructions, turn a couple pages ahead to "Renaming the Nodes and Setting up The Network." When that step is completed, refer to Appendix B for a quick guide to downloading and installing the provided images.

To make it quickly apparent which node is on the screen, an image editor will be used to change the appearance of that image. Just before editing the *default.png* image, create a backup copy of it by typing the following commands on the command line:

```
cd /usr/share/backgrounds/images
cp default.png default.png_orig
cd
```

Creating a backup copy of the default image makes it easy to revert to the original quickly if your image editing does not work properly.

The Gimp

Click the Redhat icon in the bottom-left corner and choose GRAPHICS, The GIMP. The Gimp is a graphics editor with so many features that explaining all of them would require a book of its own.

You can get as creative as you wish in creating or changing the image for the desktop. The Gimp is not a difficult program to use. There is help available (press F1 for help). To open the file for the desktop background, click "FILE", "OPEN" and type in the path and filename. A few guidelines are as follows:

- Right-click the image in the Gimp editor to bring up a menu with many editing and saving options. It is easy to change the intensity of the blue so it is a lighter shade of blue for Oracle1; or as in the case of Oracle2, a light green. Try out the many options.

- For Oracle1, place the text **ORACLE1** in white on the top right and a large number 1 in white on the bottom right. Beware not to place the number too close to the bottom edge as the toolbar covers that area. Choose the desired color for your text by changing the foreground color as shown in Figure 2.4.

- Save the file as /usr/share/backgrounds/images/default.png so that your image will be seen by all users who have not changed the default desktop image.

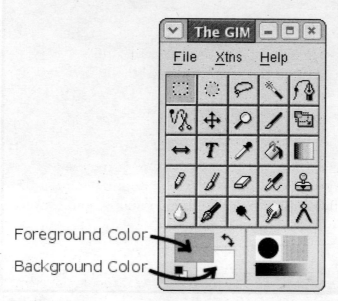

Figure 2.4: *The Gimp's Tool Palette.*

In order to view the changes made to the desktop image, it may be necessary to logout and log back in. Doing so will reload the desktop image.

Two images called bar1.png and bar2.png are included with the code depot for this book and can be used as a background for the toolbar as seen in Figure 2.5. It is acceptable to create your own images with gimp or not use any images. However, the images provided in the code depot are 100 x 100 pixels. Each has a gray background with black 1s or 2s written across it diagonally.

To use an image as the background of the toolbar, right-click the empty toolbar, choose "Properties," click the "Background Image" tab and type in the path and file name.

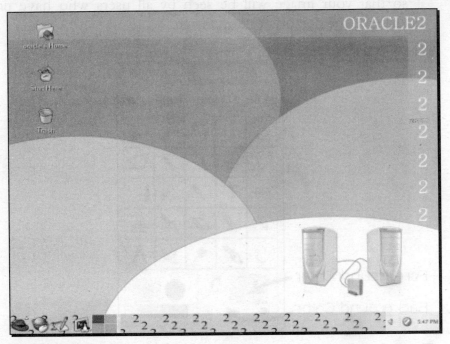

Figure 2.5: *Desktop images for oracle2 - included in the Code Depot.*

Renaming the Nodes and Setting up the Network

With the desktop images changed, it is easy to determine which node is on the screen at any time, but only when using the graphical interface gnome. The command line logins that can be accessed by typing [CTL+ALT+F1] through [CTL+ALT+F6] still appear the same on each node. To configure each node so that those logins include the node name instead of "localhost," the hostname and network settings must be configured.

Each node has two Network Interface Cards (NICs) identified by eth0 and eth1. With Fedora installed on the computers used for writing this book, eth0 was the NIC closest to the ceiling, and eth1 was the NIC closest to the floor. However, your computer hardware may produce different results.

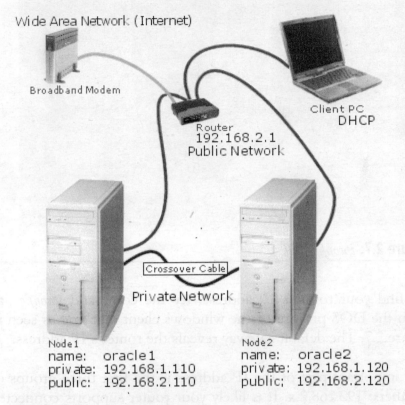

Figure 2.6: *Network configuration & node naming example.*

To assign an IP that will work for the public network (eth1), you must find the IP address of your router. Both a Microsoft Router and a Belkin Wireless/Wired Combination Router were tested in writing this book. And in each case, the router was assigned the same IP for the public network by its respective manufacturer: 192.168.2.1. Keep in mind, though, other routers may have a different IP address and thus require different IP addresses on the public network.

```
C:\WINDOWS\system32\cmd.exe                                          _ □ X

C:\Documents and Settings>ipconfig /all
Windows IP Configuration
    Host Name . . . . . . . . . . . . : DRAGON
    Primary Dns Suffix  . . . . . . . :
    Node Type . . . . . . . . . . . . : Hybrid
    IP Routing Enabled. . . . . . . . : No
    WINS Proxy Enabled. . . . . . . . : No
    DNS Suffix Search List. . . . . . : Belkin
Ethernet adapter Local Area Connection i:
    Connection-specific DNS Suffix  . : Belkin
    Description . . . . . . . . . . . : Intel(R) PRO/100
    Physical Address. . . . . . . . . : 00-07-E9-72-68-A
    Dhcp Enabled. . . . . . . . . . . : Yes
    Autoconfiguration Enabled . . . . : Yes
    IP Address. . . . . . . . . . . . : 192.168.2.3
    Subnet Mask . . . . . . . . . . . : 255.255.255.0
    Default Gateway . . . . . . . . . : 192.168.2.1
    DHCP Server . . . . . . . . . . . : 192.168.2.1
    DNS Servers . . . . . . . . . . . : 192.168.2.1
    Lease Obtained. . . . . . . . . . : Friday, April 01
    Lease Expires . . . . . . . . . . : Monday, January
C:\Documents and Settings>_
```

Figure 2.7: *ipconfig / all.*

To find your router's IP address, try the command *ipconfig* /all from the DOS prompt of the windows client machine as seen in Figure 2.7. The default gateway reveals the router's IP address.

The important part of the IP address is the first three groups of numbers: 192.168.2.x. It is likely your router supports connected devices from 192.168.2.2 to 192.168.2.255. Usually the first 30 or so addresses are reserved for DHCP, or dynamically assigned IP addresses. DHCP addresses allow for a device to be plugged into the local network. The router automatically detects and leases an IP address to the device. For this project, however, static IP addresses will be used.

> 🔔 The rest of this chapter is written with the assumption that your router's local IP address is 192.168.2.1. If it is different, you should make the appropriate changes. For example, if your router has an address of 192.168.1.1, then the public IP's for your nodes should be 192.168.1.110 and 192.168.1.120 and your private IP's should be 192.168.2.110 and 192.168.2.120. Use Table 2.1 to compare the author's configuration with your own.

	NODE NAME	NIC	IP ADDRESS	DEF. GATEWAY
Author's Configuration:	oracle1	eth0	192.168.1.110	
	oracle1	eth1	192.168.2.110	192.168.2.1
Router: 192.168.2.1	oracle2	eth0	192.168.1.120	
	oracle2	eth1	192.168.2.120	192.168.2.1
Subnet Mask for all NIC's: 255.255.255.0 – All NIC's active when computer starts.				
Your Configuration:	oracle1	eth0		
	oracle1	eth1		
Router:	oracle2	eth0		
_____	oracle2	eth1		

Table 2.1: *Table to configure the NIC cards*

Now, you need to determine which of your two network cards on each node is labeled eth1. For the computers used in writing this book, the NIC cards that were closest to the bottom of the case were assigned the label eth1 by Fedora. To be certain you are working with eth1, temporarily unplug the internal cross-over cable from the cards that is believed to be eth0 and make sure the other cards are connected to the router.

On Oracle1, open the Network Configuration Utility by clicking the "Redhat" icon in the bottom left corner of the desktop, then "System Settings," then "Network". Alternatively, launch this application by entering *redhat-config-network* in the run application applet window. A program will appear like that shown in Figure 2.9.

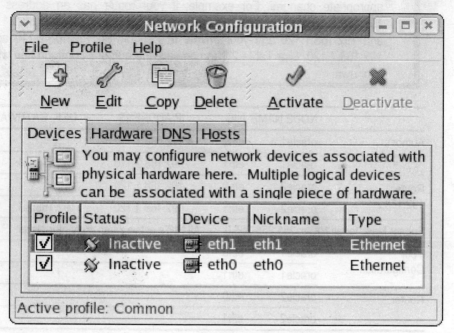

Figure 2.9: *Fedora's Network Configuration Utility.*

If the devices eth0 or eth1 are not shown, which is expected if the installer was launched with the noprobe option, click the "NEW" button to add them in with the appropriate settings as seen in Figure 2.10.

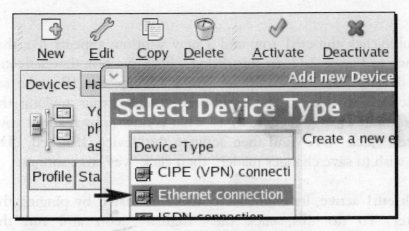

Figure 2.10: *Adding ethernet devices, necessary after a "noprobe" install.*

Figure 2.11: *Configuring eth1 for the Public Network.*

Double-click the eth1 row and a new window appears like that shown in Figure 2.11. In this dialog, check the box that activates the device when the computer starts. Change the IP to be set statically and type in the appropriate values, thus making the appropriate changes according to what is now known about your router. Click "OK" and then activate the device. If asked, "Do you wish to save changes made?" then click "yes" to continue.

With eth1 active, its connectivity must be tested by pinging the router. To do this, click the "Redhat" icon and run the application. In the window that pops up, type in gnome-terminal. From this terminal, ping the router as shown in Figure 2.12; to stop the pinging, type [control+c]. If the pings are not returned by the router, ensure that the cable to the public network is attached properly to both the NIC card and the router. If that does not work, switch the cable to the alternate NIC card to see if you actually configured that NIC instead.

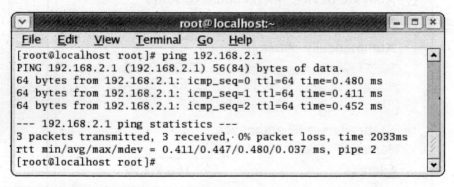

Figure 2.12: *Pinging From the gnome-terminal.*\

At this point, you have one NIC card working on Oracle1 and have identified which NIC is eth1. Now, by repeating the preceding procedure, configure Oracle2 so that its eth1 NIC is able to ping the router as well.

With the NIC cards on the public network configured, fill in the information for your network into the table in Figure 2.8. You are now ready to configure the remaining NICs.

Next, reconnect the crossover cable. Configure and activate the eth0 network card for each node using the same method used for eth1. With the private network configured, you should be able to ping the alternate node's private IP address.

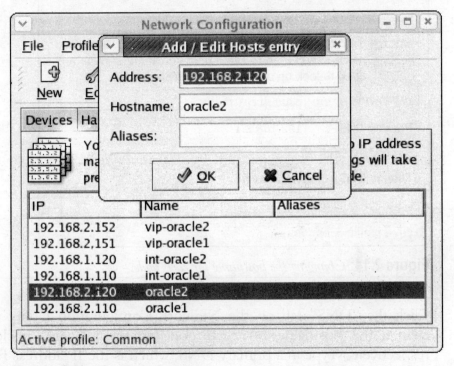

Figure 2.13: *Configure the hosts.*

Click the "Hosts" tab of the Network Configuration Utility. Click "New," and type in the address and hostname one at a time for six hosts as shown in Figure 2.13. The order is of the hosts is irrelevant. Use the IP addresses used for eth0 and eth1. vip-oracle1 and vip-oracle2 are used by the listeners to support failover in an Oracle 10g RAC. Use the prefix for your public network for the two VIP host names. Complete this step on both nodes.

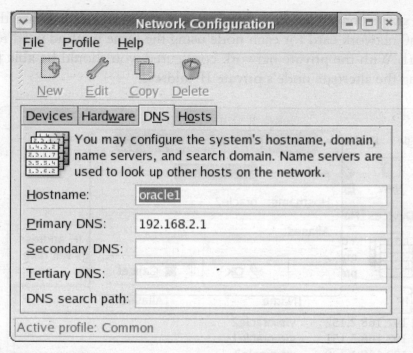

Figure 2.14: *Changing the hostname for each node.*

Click the "DNS" tab on the Network Configuration Utility to change the hostname for each node to oracle1 and oracle2 respectively. Type in a primary DNS, which is the IP address for your router. Make absolutely certain that the spelling of the hostname is the same as what was typed in for hosts in the previous step; otherwise, Fedora will become confused on the next reboot.

Once these steps are complete, click the "File" tab and SAVE. At this point, each node will become unstable. Fedora has a panic attack whenever the hostname is changed. To fix this problem, reboot each node now. Click the "Redhat" icon and then click the "logout" icon. This will bring up a dialog in which the computer can be restarted.

After rebooting each node, login and check that you can successfully ping the router, oracle1, oracle2, int-oracle1, and int-oracle2. If not, check that the entries for the hosts are correct as shown in Figure 2.13. Finally, check that the web pages are accessible. If not, it may be that the node is attempting to resolve public addresses on the private network.

Figure 2.15 demonstrates this by using the traceroute command to attempt to connect to www.oracle.com. Although the correct IP is found, the int-oracle1 connection is the first attempted hop. This will never work! If this happens, open the redhat-config-network program. Remove the default gateway address for the network card on the internal network, and ensure the default gateway is the router's IP address for the card on the public network. Save the configuration and restart the network service with the command /sbin/service network restart.

Figure 2.15: *Attempting to connect to a public address via the private network.*

When the network is completely configured, pinging the private node names, the public node names, and downloading web pages should all work. Once this is successfully configured, make a note in Figure 2.8 to remember which NIC (eth0 or eth1) is on the public network and which is on the private network. The nodes must be configured to use the same NICs (eth1 or eth2) for each network.

Ensuring All Necessary Software is Installed

The code depot for this book includes a script that, when run, will request insertion of the Fedora install CDs and will install any software that is required by Oracle. This script is also available by itself on the web.

Figure 2.16 demonstrates the use of *wget* to obtain the *ensure_installed.sh* script and then runs the script. When the first Fedora install CD is inserted, an alert window may appear asking, "Do you wish to run the /mnt/cdrom/auotrun". Answer "No" to this question. Then continue with the script.

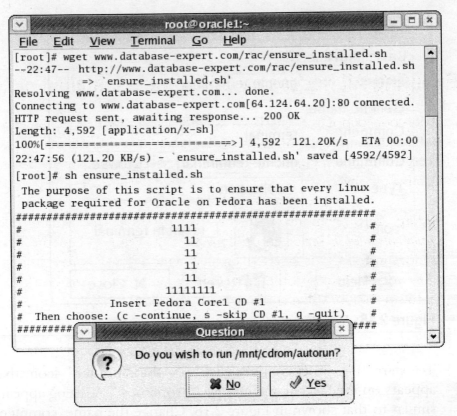

```
root@oracle1:~                          [_][□][×]

File   Edit   View   Terminal   Go   Help

[root]# wget www.database-expert.com/rac/ensure_installed.sh
--22:47-- http://www.database-expert.com/rac/ensure_installed.sh
       => `ensure_installed.sh'
Resolving www.database-expert.com... done.
Connecting to www.database-expert.com[64.124.64.20]:80 connected.
HTTP request sent, awaiting response... 200 OK
Length: 4,592 [application/x-sh]
100%[=============================>] 4,592  121.20K/s  ETA 00:00
22:47:56 (121.20 KB/s) - `ensure_installed.sh' saved [4592/4592]

[root]# sh ensure_installed.sh
 The purpose of this script is to ensure that every Linux
 package required for Oracle on Fedora has been installed.
###########################################################
#                       1111                              #
#                       11                                #
#                       11                                #
#                       11                                #
#                       11                                #
#                    11111111                             #
#            Insert Fedora Core1 CD #1                    #
#  Then choose: (c -continue, s -skip CD #1, q -quit)     #
#########                                            #####
```

Question   [×]

(?)   Do you wish to run /mnt/cdrom/autorun?

      [✖ No]   [✔ Yes]

Figure 2.16: *Running the ensure_installed.sh script.*

Configuring the Quick Launch to be Useful

Figure 2.17: *Configure the Toolbar Quick Launch*

There are two programs that will be used frequently, namely
gnome-terminal and gedit. To make the desktop easier to use,
now is a good time to change the taskbar to include these
programs.

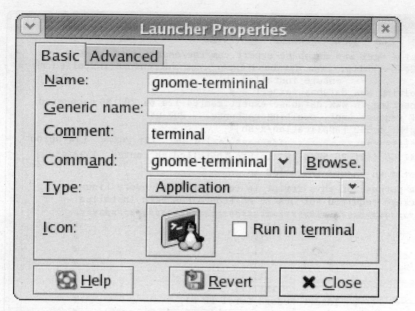

Figure 2.18: *Launcher Properties.*

To start this process, right-click on the "Printer" icon that appears on the taskbar and choose "Properties". A dialog appears similar to that shown in Figure 2.18. Change the name, comment and command to gnome-terminal. Then change the icon by clicking the "Icon" and choosing a new icon that makes sense to you for a terminal. Finally click "Close."

Repeat the above steps to change the icon that launches the mail program, but this time to launch gedit. For name, comment, and command type gedit. Change the icon to one that makes sense for a text editor.

 Now is a good time to download the code depot, especially if you wish to install the provided desktop images. Turn to Appendix B for instructions.

Conclusion

Now that Linux has been successfully installed, it is time to learn about the operating system and to configure it for an Oracle RAC install.

Fedora Linux Basics

This chapter will cover the basics of Fedora Core 1 Linux and will help you to prepare the nodes for installing Oracle software. If you are already familiar with Linux, you may prefer to skim this chapter to review only the details you need to cover.

Accessing Hard Disks

An important first step when learning a new operating system is determining how to view the contents of the disk drives and other devices such as CD ROMs and floppies.

To begin this process, launch a gnome-terminal and type the ls command. This command lists the contents of the current working directory, most likely the account's home directory, /root if logged in as root.

The ls command can be combined with a number of switches, giving it more functionality. For example, the ls –l command returns a list of files along with all of the attributes of the files. This command will not return hidden files. Use the ls –a command to return a list of all files or the ls –la command to return all files including their attributes.

The ls command can be combined with a path such as ls /etc or a filename such as ls myfile.txt or both a path and a filename. It can also be used with wildcards such as * for multi-characters, or ? for a single character.

The cd command is used to change to a different working directory. For example, cd /etc will place you into the /etc directory. The cd command alone will place you back into the home directory.

Using the ls command, you can now examine how Linux controls devices such as hard drives and CDROMs. In the directory /dev there are listings for hundreds of files that allow Linux to control devices, most of which are not in use at this time. These device files are used by Linux to pass data to and receive data from a device driver and communicate with devices. Linux uses the file /dev/hda to read from and write to the first hard disk.

If this hard disk is partitioned, it uses the /dev/hda1 file to access the first partition. Similarly, the /dev/hda2 file is used to access the second partition on the first drive.

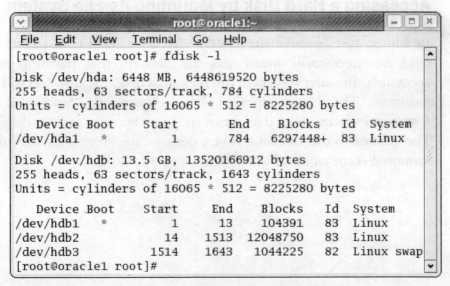

Figure 3.1: *Listing the hard disks and partitions.*

The fdisk -l command is used to list the hard disks and their subsequent partitions on the system. This command will list all partitions, even those that are not mounted or formatted.

In the example shown in Figure 3.1, the first line reports that hard disk /dev/hda is 6,448 megabytes. The second line reports that it has 784 cylinders. The third line reports each cylinder is 8,225,280 bytes. Below the third line, the partitions are listed, which in this case is just one, /dev/hda1.

This partition starts on cylinder 1 and ends on cylinder 784, the final cylinder. A second drive, /dev/hdb is also listed. It has 13.5 gigabytes and three partitions: /dev/hdb1, /dev/hdb2, and /dev/hdb3. The start cylinder, end cylinder, and file system for each partition are listed.

Accessing a Hard Disk by Mounting its File System

In Linux, just because the system detects a hard disk partition does not necessarily mean that the files on that partition are accessible. In order to access the files on a disk, the disk has to be mounted. This brings up the obvious question, "Since the ls command works, does that mean files can be accessed on disk?" The answer to this question is yes, because the system has already mounted some or all of the partitions on the disks.

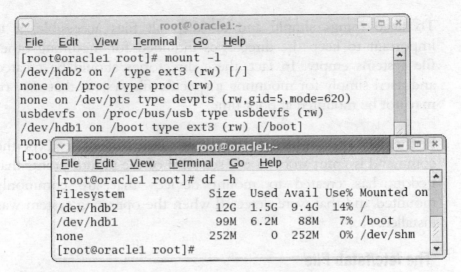

Figure 3.2: *Viewing what file systems are mounted.*

To determine what partitions or devices are mounted at any time, use either the mount –l or the df –h command as shown in Figure 3.2. In this example, the partition /dev/hdb2 is mounted on the mount-point /, and the partition /dev/hdb1 is mounted on the mount-point /boot. The swap partition /dev/hdb3 is not mounted because swap partitions are handled differently by the operating system. Note that the df -h command reports the used and available disk space on each mounted file system.

What is a Mount-Point?

To access a file system on a device such as a hard drive or floppy drive, the file system must be mounted. To mount a new file system, a directory must exist in the current file system. That directory does not have to be empty; there can be files within it even subdirectories. However, once a different file system is mounted to that directory, the files and subdirectories within that directory will become unavailable until the new file system is un-mounted.

To keep things simple and to keep all files accessible, it is important to keep the directories intended for mounting other file systems empty. In fact, these directories should be created and used simply for mounting a specific file system that may or may not be mounted at boot time.

Fedora has a few mount-points already created for use. Type the command ls /mnt and you will see a list of the mount-points that Fedora has created to mount devices that are commonly mounted and that were detected when the operating system was installed.

The /etc/fstab File

The /etc/fstab file is a text file that tells Fedora what file systems to mount on boot. It also associates certain devices to certain mount-points, effectively abbreviating the command for mounting those devices. To view this file, type the command more /etc/fstab as shown in Figure 3.3.

```
root@oracle1:~
File   Edit   View   Terminal   Go   Help
[root@oracle1 root]# more /etc/fstab
LABEL=/          /             ext3      defaults         1 1
LABEL=/boot      /boot         ext3      defaults         1 2
none             /dev/pts      devpts    gid=5,mode=620   0 0
none             /proc         proc      defaults         0 0
none             /dev/shm      tmpfs     defaults         0 0
/dev/hdb3        swap          swap      defaults         0 0
/dev/cdrom       /mnt/cdrom    udf,iso9660 noauto,owner,kudzu,1
/dev/cdrom1      /mnt/cdrom1   udf,iso9660 noauto,owner,kudzu,1
/dev/fd0         /mnt/floppy   auto      noauto,owner,kudzu 0 0
[root@oracle1 root]#
```

Figure 3.3: *//etc//fstab file contents*

The contents of the /etc/fstab file are listed in six columns, delimited by white-space, namely device, mount-point, file-system type, options, dump, and file-system check order. The details for each of these columns can be found in the manual page for the /etc/fstab file. Type the man fstab command to enter a manual page, and type q to exit a manual page.

In the example shown in Figure 3.3, the device with label "/" is mounted at the mount-point /, and the device with label "/boot" is mounted at /boot. There are two CDROMs and one floppy that have each been assigned its own mount-point.

Mounting a File System with the Mount Command

Figure 3.4 shows an example of mounting a file system using the full syntax and another example using the abbreviated syntax. The line beginning with ### is commented out. It is used to illustrate the various parts of the mount command.

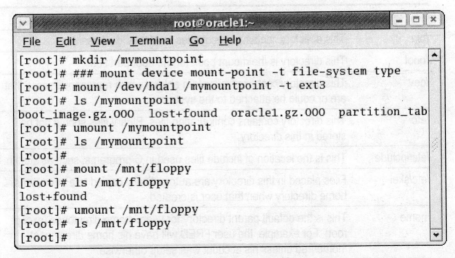

```
root@oracle1:~
File  Edit  View  Terminal  Go  Help
[root]# mkdir /mymountpoint
[root]# ### mount device mount-point -t file-system type
[root]# mount /dev/hda1 /mymountpoint -t ext3
[root]# ls /mymountpoint
boot_image.gz.000  lost+found  oracle1.gz.000  partition_tab
[root]# umount /mymountpoint
[root]# ls /mymountpoint
[root]#
[root]# mount /mnt/floppy
[root]# ls /mnt/floppy
lost+found
[root]# umount /mnt/floppy
[root]# ls /mnt/floppy
[root]#
```

Figure 3.4: *Using the mount command to mount a file syste*

Only a device or partition listed in the configuration file /etc/fstab can be mounted with the abbreviated syntax such as shown for mounting the floppy drive.

The umount command is used to un-mount a file system (note the missing "n"). Always un-mount a file system before removing a floppy or CD; Linux does not gracefully handle unexpected file system removal.

File System Hierarchy Standard

Fedora and other Redhat distributions have a standardized file system that makes finding different kinds of files predictable. This standard is referred to by Redhat as the File System Hierarchy Standard. Table 3.1 lists many of the directories that are found in the main partition of Fedora, along with the purpose for each one.

Directory	Purpose
/	This directory is the mount point for the main system partition.
/bin	This directory contains executables available to all users.
/boot	This directory is the mount point for the boot partition.
/dev	This directory contains file system entries which represent devices that are or could be attached to the system.
/etc	This directory contains configuration files. Binary files should not be stored in this directory.
/etc/include	This is the location of include files used in C programs, such as stdio.h.
/etc/skel	Files placed in this directory are automatically copied to a new user's home directory when that user is created.
/home	This is the default parent directory for users' home directories (except root). For example, the user FRED will have his home directory at /home/fred unless his account was setup otherwise.
/lib	This directory contains libraries needed to execute the binaries stored in /bin and /sbin.
/mnt	This directory contains mount points for temporarily mounted file systems such as CDROMS and floppy disks.
/opt	This directory contains subdirectories for application software that has been installed by users.

Directory	Purpose
/proc	This directory contains files that extract information from or send information to the kernel.
/root	This directory is the root user's home directory.
/sbin	This directory contains executables to be used by the root user. It also contains files that are necessary when booting the system.
/tmp	This directory is used to store temporary files.
/usr	This directory contains files that can be shared between the users of the system.
/usr/local	This directory can be used by the system administrator to install software.
/var	This directory is used to allow programs to spool data, write log files, write temporary files, etc.
~/	This is an abbreviation for the user's home directory.

Table 3.1: *Directories found in the main partition of Fedora*

The Proc File System

The proc file system is a virtual file system that is mounted at boot time. It is a virtual file system because it does not refer to a physical storage device such as a disk partition. Its purpose is to allow the user to communicate with the kernel. Parameters can be sent to the kernel while the system is running through virtual files on the proc file system, and information about the system at runtime can be obtained from virtual files in the proc file system.

An important example of using the proc file system can be seen in the command cat /proc/swaps, which returns the current usage of the swap space. Another example is the top command, which starts an ongoing process that monitors CPU and memory usage. The top process gets its information from the proc file system. Type 'q' to quit the top process.

System Configuration Files

For the most part, the Linux operating system and the programs installed on it hold their settings in text files. In the previous chapter, the redhat-config-network program was used to configure the network. This program saves changes by writing to text configuration files. Table 3.2 describes many of the configuration files used to configure Fedora Linux.

PATH AND CONFIGURATION FILE	PURPOSE
/etc/bashrc	System wide aliases and functions. This script is run when a user logs into a bash terminal, the default terminal for all users unless set up otherwise.
/etc/fstab	Configures file systems that Linux will attempt to mount on startup. Also lists mount-points for devices allowing them to be mounted with an abbreviated command.
/etc/group	Lists what groups are on the operating system and what users are members of each group.
/etc/grub.conf	The boot loader configuration file.
/etc/hosts	This file is used to resolve host names on the network. It is accessed before checking DNS.
/etc/hosts.equiv	Specifies trusted users on remote systems that can execute commands on the local system. Requires the xinetd deamon to be configured and running.
/etc/inittab	The first configuration file run after booting. Defines the default run-level after boot. Run-level 3 boots to a command prompt that supports multiple logins, with network access. Run-level 5 boots to a graphical user interface.
/etc/modules.conf	Kernel modules configuration file.
/etc/mtab	This configuration file lists what is mounted currently. It should not be edited with a text editor. Use the mount command instead.
/etc/passwd	The system password file, lists user information
/etc/profile	System wide environment setup startup programs for logins.

PATH AND CONFIGURATION FILE	PURPOSE
/etc/rc.local	This is the final script run when the system is started. It is a common practice for the administrator to add commands to this file that should be run when starting up the node.
/etc/resolv.conf	This file configures where Linux will look for a name server.
/etc/shadow	Account passwords for users to login are encrypted and stored in this file. This file is only readable by the root user.
/etc/sysconfig/network	This file contains the hostname for the node.
/etc/sysctl.conf	Kernel configuration file.

Table 3.2: *Configuration files used to configure Fedora Linux*

User Configuration Files

A number of configuration files can be found in each user's home directory, including root's home directory /root. These files are "hidden" from the ls command; a feat accomplished by naming the files with a period as the first character, as the filename. The command ls ~/ -a will return a list of all files in the home directory, including hidden files.

The /etc/skel directory is used to store files that are automatically copied into a user's home directory when that user is created by root. To make a change to the default configuration files used for all users created from this point forward, simply edit or create a file in the /etc/skel directory.

Table 3.3 explains the purpose of the most common user configuration files.

PATH AND CONFIGURATION FILE	PURPOSE
~/.bash_logout	User specific logout routine.

PATH AND CONFIGURATION FILE	PURPOSE
~/.bash_profile	User specific environment & startup programs. This file is only run when a user logs in. It is not run when the su command is run to switch user logins.
~/.bashrc	User specific aliases and functions. This file defines aliases and functions. It is not necessary to logout of the gnome windows manager after editing this file to make changes effective. Simply open a new terminal window.
~/.emacs	User specific emacs text editor configuration.

Table 3.3: *Most common user configuration files.*

Linux File Ownership and Permissions

A characteristic of most operating systems is file ownership and permissions. File permissions help to keep the operating system safe from accidental or intentional mishaps. To view a file's ownership and permissions, use the ls -l command as shown in Figure 3.5.

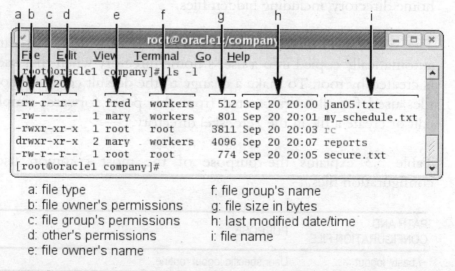

a: file type
b: file owner's permissions
c: file group's permissions
d: other's permissions
e: file owner's name

f: file group's name
g: file size in bytes
h: last modified date/time
i: file name

Figure 3.5: *Listing file permissions.*

The first character (pointer a) in the listing indicates whether the file is a regular file (with a dash) or a directory (with a letter d). The next three groups of characters (pointers b,c,d) indicate the read (r), write (w), and execute (x) permissions of the file's owner, group and all other users respectively. The other items in the listing (pointers e through i) are self-explanatory.

As seen in Figure 3.5, the file jan05.txt is set so that the owner has read and write permissions, while all other users have read only permission. The file my_schedule.txt has been set so that for example Mary can read or write the file, but no one else can read or write to it. The file rc can be read or executed by anyone, but only its owner can write over it.

The file a user creates has default permissions according to the way that it was created. In most cases, the permissions will be set so that the owner can read and write but all others will have read permission only. File permissions and ownership can be changed after a file is created.

Changing a File's Ownership

Only the root user can use the command chown to change a file's owner and group. The syntax is easy: chown user:group /path/filename. The root user can also add the switch –R to make the chown command recursive for all files in a given directory, including files in subdirectories.

A user other than root cannot change a file's ownership, but the user can change the group of a file he owns to any group of which he is a member by using the *chgrp* command, as in: chgrp group /path/filename.

Changing a File's Permissions or "Mode"

Use the chmod command to change a file's permissions (also known as its mode). There are two syntaxes available for use with chmod: symbolic and absolute. The following table lists a few examples of each. Note that when the symbolic syntax is used, no spaces are permitted after the commas when listing the permissions assigned to user, group and others.

SYMBOLIC SYNTAX	ABSOLUTE SYNTAX	DESCRIPTION
chmod ugo=rwx filename	chmod 777 filename	Allows user, group, others to read, write and execute.
chmod u=rw,g=r,o=r filename	chmod 644 filename	Allows user to read and write, group and others to read.
chmod u=rwx,g-rwx,o-rwx file	chmod 700 file	Allows user to read, write and execute, group and others are denied any access to the file.
chmod u+x filename		Adds execute permission to file owner without effecting other permissions.

Table 3.5: *Symbolic Syntax*

The symbolic syntax can be used to add or remove permissions without effecting other permissions as they are.

The absolute syntax redefines all permissions at once according to bits. The following table gives an example of how the 744 bits are computed to determine read, write, execute for user, read for group and read for others:

MODE	User	Group	Others
Read	400 *	40 *	4 *
Write	200 *	20	2

MODE	User		Group		Others
Execute	100 *		10		1
Sum	700	+ 40		+ 4	= 744

Table 3.4: *How 744 bits are computed*

The *chmod* command can be combined with the switch –R and a wildcard to make it recursive (for example chmod u=rw,g=r,o=r –R *), so that it changes the mode of all files in that directory and all subdirectories as well.

To get more information about chmod, type the command man chmod which will bring up the manual for chmod, and type q to exit the manual.

Changing the Default Permissions for Newly Created Files

Just as *chmod* is used to change the mode of files that exist, the umask command is used to set up a mask which forces newly created files during the current session to take on a specific set of permissions. To view the current mask, run the umask –S command. The symbolic and absolute syntaxes are available for use with the umask command.

The symbolic syntax is easy to use. For example, the command umask u=rwx,g=,o= forces files created from this point forward to allow the file owner (user) to read, write and execute; whereas members of the group, or others cannot read, write or execute. The absolute syntax requires a bit of math to make it work. For example the command umask u=rwx,g=,o= can also be accomplished with the command umask 077. The numbers 077 are derived by subtracting the value that would be obtained with the chmod command from the maximum value possible, 777. So, to change the mask to allow read and write to user, and read to group and others, you would run the command umask 133 and then check it with umask -S.

To set a default mask for future logins, the umask command can be added to the user's ~/.bash_profile.

The vi Text Editor

The text editor *vi*, pronounced "vee-eye," can be called from the command line, and it stays on the command line. This powerful editor is easy to use, but it is not intuitive. You must know the commands to make it work or at the very least know how to look them up. Pointing and clicking will get you nowhere. Fortunately, just memorizing a few basic commands will make it quite useful.

In Fedora Linux, the original *vi* has been replaced with "vi improved," launched on the command line with *vi* or *vim*. The syntax to open a file in the vim editor is *vi </path/filename>*. If the file exists, it will open that file; if it does not exist, it will create the file. If you do not name a file, the editor will run without editing a named file until what has been created is saved.

The *vi* editor utilizes three modes: command mode, edit mode and ex mode. Open the editor with the *vi* command to begin in the command mode. In this mode, the editor can be given commands that it will follow such as write (:w), quit (:q), quit without saving (:q!), replace (:R), or find (:/<text_to_find>). Most important of all are the commands help (:h) and help about a particular subject (:h subject).

To enter the edit mode, you can press the "i" key to begin inserting text or the a key to append text. Type in the text desired. The up, down, left and right arrows will work as expected. Exit the edit mode by pressing [Esc], and you are ready to type a command for *vi* to respond to.

Vi's ex mode (extended mode) is beyond the scope of this book. For more information on *vi*, visit the vim website at http://www.vim.org.

The gedit Text Editor

The text editor *gedit* is extremely easy to use because it is intuitive. It can be called from a command line as long as the terminal is open in an XWindows environment. To edit a particular file, type the command *gedit* </path/filename>. Of course, the *gedit* editor can also be called from the command line without naming a file. If the *gedit* button has been added to the taskbar as described at the end of chapter two, simply clicking this button will launch the *gedit* text editor.

So the obvious question is, "if *gedit* can be used, why use *vi*?" The answer is that *vi* can be launched from and remain within a command line context, important when using telnet or ssh to connect remotely. Therefore, it is important to become familiar with *vi*.

Run Levels

"Run level" is the term used to describe the mode that the operating system is running in at any given time. The list is easy to understand and remember. Fedora boots to run level 5 by default, which means it will boot into a graphical user interface. The following list describes the available run levels:

Run Level Description
    0 Halt – Turn off the computer
    1 Single user mode
    2 Multiuser, without networking
    3 Full multiuser mode, with networking

4 Unused
5 X11 – Graphical User Interface
6 Reboot

The file /etc/inittab sets the run level at boot. The command *grep* "default:" /etc/inittab will display the line in this file which sets the default run level.

The *init* command can be used to change the run level, which will require a shutdown or reboot. Use the command *init* 0 to shutdown a node. Use the command *init* 6 to reboot. This command must be run as root.

Refer to Appendix E for instructions on changing the default run level to 3 in order to launch different windows managers.

Starting and Stopping Services

Linux runs programs in the background called services or daemons. Use the service command to start or stop a service or to view a list of all the services and their corresponding statuses. Examples of the service command are as follows:

start the vsftpd service (ftp server daemon):
service vsftpd start

stop the vsftpd service:
service vsftpd stop

restart the vsftpd service:
service vsftpd restart

view a list of services and the status of each one:
service —status -all

Turning a Service On/Off

When a Linux server boots up, it lists all of the services it is starting (type [alt+d] when the graphical interface appears). Many of those services are unnecessary for this Oracle Project and certainly slow the machine down at least slightly. With all of those services to start, booting up can take an unbearably long time.

Use the *chkconfig* command to change the operating system configuration so that a given service starts or does not start at boot time. The *sendmail* service is the best example of a service that does not need to be started at boot time. It can easily take 5 minutes just to start that one service. The following are a number of examples of how to use *chkconfig* to toggle *sendmail* to turn on and off:

list statuses of each service
chkconfig —list

list one service
chkconfig —list sendmail

configure so that sendmail never starts on boot
chkconfig sendmail off

configure so that sendmail starts when booting

to runlevel 3
chkconfig —level 3 sendmail on

For this project, the following services can be turned off with chkconfig to speed up the boot process and lighten the load on the system. If you install the author's suggested list instead of "everything," then only the sendmail and PCMCIA will be installed.

```
chkconfig sendmail off     # email subsystem
chkconfig pcmcia off       # support for laptop pcmcia cards
chkconfig hpoj off         # HP printer drivers
chkconfig spamassassin off # spam filter
chkconfig privoxy off      # web proxy server
chkconfig canna off        # Japanese language support
chkconfig FreeWnn off      # Japanese language support
```

Command Line Basics

The command line or shell prompt used by Linux offers a wide range of commands. Appendix A lists many commands that will be used as you install and administer Oracle on Linux. There are a number of shells available on Linux. The default shell or command line interpreter is BASH. All of the work done in this project is completed in the BASH shell. Changing shells is unnecessary and not recommended for this project.

Variables and Environmental Variables

A number of variables are used by the Bash shell for its configuration. For example the prompt itself is defined by the variable PS1, which by default equals '[\u@\h \W]\$ '. This odd group of symbols is interpreted by the shell which outputs the prompt that is normally seen when a terminal is open. That prompt can be changed. To save space, many of the screen-shots captured for this book use a shorter prompt. This is done by making the variable PS1 equal to '[\u]\$ '.

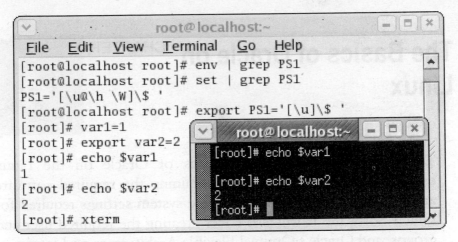

Figure 3.6: *A variable vs. an environmental variable.*

Figure 3.6 illustrates the difference between a variable and an environmental variable. To begin, the *env* command returns a list of all environmental variables which is piped into or combined with *grep* PS1. Nothing is found. Next, the set command, which lists all variables, is piped into *grep* PS1. This time, PS1 is found. Therefore, PS1 is a variable, but not an environmental variable.

To make PS1 an environmental variable, the export command is used. Next, var1 and var2 are created, but only var2 is exported into the environment. Then an xterm is launched. Xterm is a child process of the gnome-terminal. It inherits only the environmental variables PS1 and var2.

Environmental variables are important to the Oracle Database Administrator. They are used to pass information to the Oracle processes that are launched from the command line.

Conclusion

It is time to proceed with learning about Oracle software and installing it on our nodes to support a RAC configuration.

The Basics of Oracle on Linux

This chapter will cover the basics of Oracle on the Linux operating system. It will cover obtaining the required software and burning it to CDs, as well as the system settings required for Oracle Software. It will also cover creating the required user and groups, and Oracle's Optimal Flexible Architecture on Linux.

Obtaining the Software

Although many software components are required to accomplish the goals of this book, all software can be obtained without cost. Table 4.1 describes each software component and the website address which offers it for download.

SOFTWARE AND WEBSITE	NOTES
Oracle9i Database Release 2 Enterprise & Standard Edition for Linux http://otn.oracle.com	Download the following three files to the node with the most free local diskspace: ship_9204_linux_disk1.cpio.gz ship_9204_linux_disk2.cpio.gz ship_9204_linux_disk3.cpio.gz Downloading Oracle software will require login to your OTN account. If you do not have an account, you can sign up free of charge.
Oracle Database 10g Release 1 (10.1.0.3) for Linux x86 http://otn.oracle.com	ship.db.lnx32.cpio.gz

SOFTWARE AND WEBSITE	NOTES
Oracle Cluster Ready Services Release 1 (10.1.0.3) for Linux x86 http://otn.oracle.com	ship.crs.lnx32.cpio.gz
Oracle Database 10g Release 2 (10.2.0.1.0) for Linux x86 http://otn.oracle.com	10201_database_linux32.zip
Oracle Clusterware Release 2 (10.2.0.1.0) for Linux x86 http://otn.oracle.com	10201_clusterware_linux32.zip
Modified Linux Kernel for Firewire http://oss.oracle.com/projects/ firewire/files/RedHat/ RHEL3/i386/	kernel-2.4.21-27.0.2.ELorafw1.i686.rpm
Oracle Cluster File System http://oss.oracle.com/projects/ ocfs/files/RedHat/RHEL3/i386/	ocfs-2.4.21-EL-1.0.14-1.i686.rpm ocfs-support-1.0.10-1.i386.rpm ocfs-tools-1.0.10-1.i386.rpm
Automatic Storage Management For Oracle 10g http://www.oracle.com/ technology/tech/linux/ asmlib/index.html	oracleasmlib-1.0.0-1.i386.rpm oracleasm-support-1.0.3-1.i386.rpm oracleasm-2.4.21-EL-1.0.3-1.i686.rpm
Rlwrap http://utopia.knoware.nl/~hlub/ uck/rlwrap/	Sqlplus on Linux has no command line history feature. This software adds the history feature.
Code Depot www.database-expert.com/rac/ code_depot.zip	There are items in the code depot that are required for this project. See Appendix B for more information.

Table 4.1: *Software components & websites that offer it for download*

Figure 4.1 demonstrates using the *cksum* command to verify that a downloaded file is complete and uncorrupted. The value returned should be compared with the value posted on Oracle's download page. After it is verified, the *gunzip* command is used to extract the file. Once this is complete, the *cpio* command is used to extract the archived files. Note that 10g release 2 files are simply unzipped.

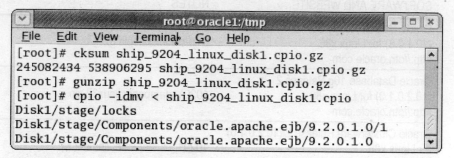

Figure 4.1: *Verifying and unpacking an Oracle install file.*

The author suggests using the gnome-toaster to burn the install files to a CD. The application can be launched from the command line with the gtoaster command. Gnome-Toaster is very easy to use. Simply highlight the files and directories to be burned that are located on the upper right of the screen and drag them into the lower right portion of the screen. Then click the "Record" button. Burn the files and directories starting inside the directory "disk1" as shown in Figure 4.2.

Figure 4.2: *Burning the 9i install disk one with Gnome Toaster.*

The author suggests creating one CD with the files for the modified kernel, *ocfs*, *oracleasm*, *rhwrap* and the Code Depot.

Installing the Modified Kernel

A modified kernel is necessary in order to use the external disk as shared storage. As root, copy the modified kernel file from the CD to the /tmp directory. Change directories to /tmp, and then use the rpm command with the --force switch to install this package as shown in Figure 4.3.

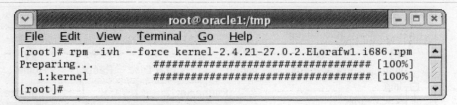

Figure 4.3: *Installing the modified kernel.*

Once the kernel is installed, open the /etc/grub.conf file with a text editor and change the line that reads default=1 to default=0. This will make the new kernel the default kernel. Optionally, change the title to include the words "Firewire for RAC" and include the node name as shown in Figure 4.4.

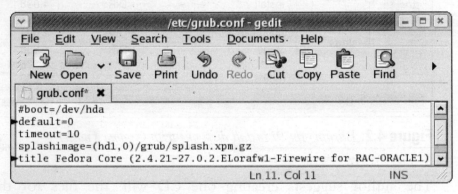

Figure 4.4: *Editing /etc/grub.conf.*

System Settings Required to run Oracle Software

Located in the Code Depot for this book (see Appendix B) is a script called *os_prep.sh*. This script should be run as the root user on each node. It will automatically write each of the settings described in the following section to the necessary system configuration files.

SYSTEM SETTING	DESCRIPTION
kernel.shmni (leave at default)	The maximum number of system-wide shared memory segments.
kernel.shmmax =2147483648	The maximum size of each shared memory segment. It should be set to a minimum of half the real memory. Setting it at 2 gigabytes will not cause trouble even if there is minimal RAM installed. It is saved in file /etc/sysctl.conf.
kernel.shmall (leave at default)	Defines the maximum amount of shared memory that may be in use at any time on the system.
kernel.shmseg (leave at default)	Defines the maximum number of shared memory segments to which a single process can attach.
Semmsl	Maximum number of semaphores per set.
Semmns	Total number of semaphores in the system.
Semopm	Maximum number of operations per semop call.
Semmni	Maximum number of semaphore sets.
The previous four semaphore parameters are saved in /etc/sysctl.conf using the following syntax, delimited by white space: ### kernel.sem=semmsl semmns semopm semmni kernel.sem=250 32000 100 128	
fs.file-max = 65536	Determines the maximum number of files that any single process can open. It is saved in file /etc/sysctl.conf.
net.core.rmem_default=262144	Each network socket is allocated a send buffer for outbound packets and a receive socket for inbound packets. To support high data rates required for Oracle's cache fusion, these four parameters are increased. It is saved in file /etc/sysctl.conf.
net.core.wmem_default=262144	
net.core.rmem_max=262144	
net.core.wmem_max=262144	

SYSTEM SETTING	DESCRIPTION
ulimit –u 16384	Sets the maximum number of processes that a user can start. The Oracle user starts the database, which requires a high limit. It is saved in file /etc/rc.local.

Table 4.2: *System settings and descriptions*

A few system settings are specific to a RAC on a Firewire configuration. The following table lists those settings. These settings are also included in the *os_prep.sh* script.

System Setting	Description
options sbp2 sbp2_exclusive_login=0 post-install sbp2 insmod sd_mod post-remove sbp2 rmmod sd_mod	Settings specific to the kernel modified for dual logging on the firewire drive. It is saved in the file /etc/modules.conf.

Table 4.3: *RAC specific settings on Firewire confiruration*

Running the os_prep.sh Script

Run the *os_prep.sh* script as shown in Figure 4.5. When the script has finished, use the init 6 command to reboot the node. Afterward, proceed to the next node and follow the same steps to install the modified kernel. Run the *os_prep.sh* script and reboot.

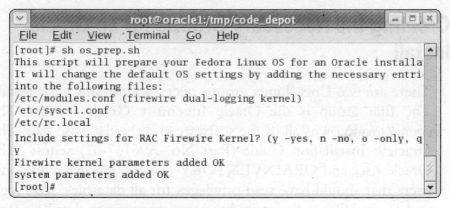

```
root@oracle1:/tmp/code_depot

 File   Edit   View   Terminal   Go   Help
[root]# sh os_prep.sh
This script will prepare your Fedora Linux OS for an Oracle installa
It will change the default OS settings by adding the necessary entri
into the following files:
/etc/modules.conf (firewire dual-logging kernel)
/etc/sysctl.conf
/etc/rc.local

Include settings for RAC Firewire Kernel? (y -yes, n -no, o -only, q
y
Firewire kernel parameters added OK
system parameters added OK
[root]#
```

Figure 4.5: *Running the os_prep.sh script.*

Verifying the External Drive

With the modified kernel installed, the *os_prep.sh* run, and each node rebooted, the external drive should now be available to each node. The commands shown in Figure 4.6 are used to verify that a given node has detected the external drive. If the external drive has been partitioned, the fdisk –l | grep sd command will return one line for the disk and one line for each partition. If the external drive is not detected, which is common for a first boot to the new kernel, another reboot of the node in question will usually fix the problem.

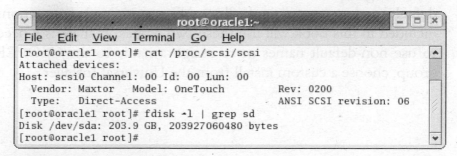

```
root@oracle1:~

 File   Edit   View   Terminal   Go   Help
[root@oracle1 root]# cat /proc/scsi/scsi
Attached devices:
Host: scsi0 Channel: 00 Id: 00 Lun: 00
  Vendor: Maxtor   Model: OneTouch        Rev: 0200
  Type:   Direct-Access                   ANSI SCSI revision: 06
[root@oracle1 root]# fdisk -l | grep sd
Disk /dev/sda: 203.9 GB, 203927060480 bytes
[root@oracle1 root]#
```

Figure 4.6: *Verify the modified kernel.*

Creating the Necessary Groups for an Oracle Install

There are two Unix/Linux groups necessary for an Oracle install. The first group is the Oracle Inventory Group - *oinstall*. The *oinstall* group owns all of the software and the database files. The Oracle9i Installation Guide (Part No. A96167-01) states, "The Oracle user and ORAINVENTORY (*oinstall*) group are the only users that should have read privileges for all data files, redo logs, and control files to maintain discretionary access to data."

The second group is the OSDBA Group - dba. This group is used to identify users with SYSDBA database privilege. Members of this group can login to the database with SYSDBA privilege using operating system authentication.

A third group, the OSOPER group - oper, is an optional group and will not be used in this book. The OSOPER group is used to allow a user to connect to the database with SYSOPER database privilege using operating system authentication.

Any name could be used for the ORAINVENTORY and OSDBA groups. For the sake of simplicity, this book will use the default names *oinstall* and dba. All scripts and instructions included in this book will use these two names. If there is a need to use non-default names or to assign a name to the OSOPER group, choose a custom install from the Universal Installer.

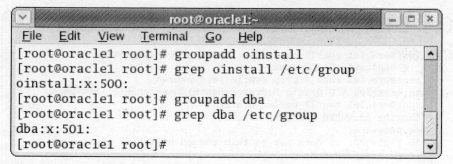

Figure 4.7: *Adding the oinstall and dba groups.*

Adding a group is very simple. From the command line, use the *groupadd* command as shown in Figure 4.7. Use the grep command to verify that the group was added to the /etc/group file. The *grep* command searches through a text file to find a particular string and returns the lines where the string is found.

Creating the Oracle Software Owner

A single user must own the Oracle software. The default name for that user is "oracle." Figure 4.8 shows the *useradd* command used to create the Oracle user with the *oinstall* group as his primary group and *dba* as a secondary group. Use the *passwd* command to change the password of the Oracle account. Linux may complain that the password does not contain enough different characters, but it should accept the new password anyway.

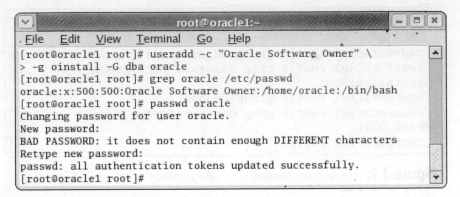

Figure 4.8: *Creating the Oracle user.*

Fedora Linux offers a GUI tool that makes administering operating system users and groups simple. The redhat-config-users command launches the Redhat User Manager as shown in Figure 4.9.

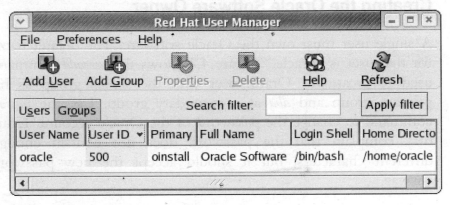

Figure 4.9: *The Redhat User Manager.*

Setting up rsh

Oracle uses the remote shell service to run commands on both nodes during the software install. Although *rsh* is not secure, it is the only option for Oracle 9i. Oracle 10g installs can use either *rsh* or *ssh*, the secure version of remote shell. Run the commands shown in Figure 4.10 to set up *rsh*. As a safeguard measure, the kerberos version of *rsh* is renamed to ensure that the standard version is used in its place. Do not be concerned if Linux reports "No such file." This would simply indicate that kerberos is not installed.

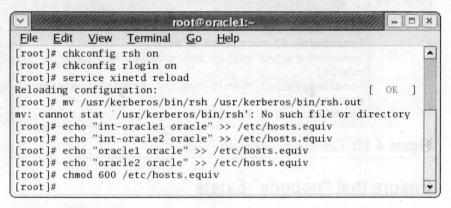

Figure 4.10: *Setting up rhs.*

Once *rsh* has been started on each node, it must be tested. The Oracle user is set up to use *rsh*. Figure 4.11 demonstrates switching to the Oracle user with the *su* command, then running the hostname command on the remote node via each network connection. This test should be run on each node as shown in Figure 4.11.

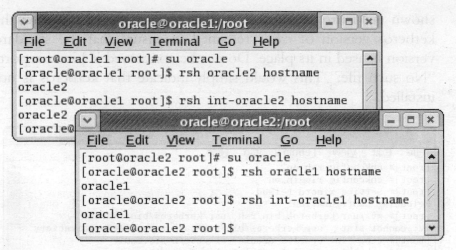

Figure 4.11: *Testing rsh from Each Node.*

Ensure that "nobody" Exists

Ensure that the user:group combination "nobody" exists as seen in Figure 4.12. This user:group should have been included with the Linux install. Oracle software will assign various files to this user and group. If the user and group do not exist, switch to root and add it with the command, /usr/sbin/useradd nobody.

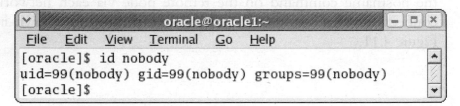

Figure 4.12: *Verify that the "nobody" user and group are included.*

Setting Oracle Environmental Variables

In order to accomplish an Oracle install successfully, certain environmental variables are required. The following table lists the variables that are frequently set when using and installing Oracle Software.

ENVIRONMENTAL VARIABLE	DESCRIPTION
$LD_ASSUME_KERNEL	This variable must be set in order to run many of the Oracle tools on Linux such as Universal Installer, dbca or netmgr.
$LD_LIBRARY_PATH	This variable allows many Oracle programs to find shared object library files.
$ORACLE_BASE	This variable is required to perform an install of Oracle software. It is used to indicate the base directory for all versions of Oracle software. Unless the administrator indicates otherwise, the oraInventory directory is located at $ORACLE_BASE/oraInventory, and is the location in which Oracle catalogs its many installed components.
$ORACLE_HOME	Setting the $ORACLE_HOME is not necessary for a successful install. However, setting it will pre-determine the value displayed for a home directory which can then be edited. After Oracle software is installed, this variable helps Oracle find files. For example, to make a database connection, Oracle will look for the tnsnames.ora file in $ORACLE_HOME/network/admin, and $ORACLE_HOME is required to run many programs such as SQLPLUS and RMAN.
$ORACLE_SID	When this variable is set, the user does not need to type in a SID name in the connect string. For example, sqlplus system/password@my_db can be shortened to sqlplus system/password. Although it is possible to set $ORACLE_SID in the .bash_profile as a default, it is not necessary. It can be set on the fly with the racenv script.
$PATH	This variable is used by Linux to find executables. For example, in order to run sqlplus from a command prompt without typing in the entire path, you must include its directory path in this variable.

Table 4.4: *Variables frequently set when using/installing Oracle*

Setting Default Environmental Variables for the Oracle User

When a user logs into Linux, a few scripts are run to set things up. One such script is the *.bash_profile* script. Use the *gedit ~oracle/.bash_profile* command to open Oracle's login script. Edit it so that the lines shown in Figure 4.13 are appended to the text.

The export command is used to set an environmental variable. To refer to a variable that has been set in a script or a command, the variable must be preceded with a dollar sign. It is a common practice in BASH scripting to type variables in upper case letters. Remember, Linux is case sensitive, so $oracle_home is not the same variable as $ORACLE_HOME.

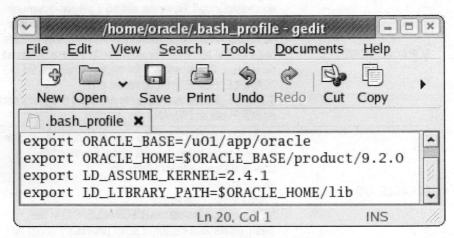

Figure 4.13: *Editing Oracle's login script.*

Using the su Command from Oracle's Login

With the *~oracle/.bash_profile* file in place, the environmental variables used by Oracle software will be in place. On occasion, the *su* command will be used to switch to the root user. Doing so will make the root login a child process of the Oracle login, and thus, the environmental variables will be inherited.

However, root's standard $PATH variable, the one root gets when root logs in directly, will not be there. Instead, root will get the Oracle user's $PATH variable, which is different. Thus, after using the *su* command to switch to root, commands such as chkconfig will need to include the full path: /sbin/chkconfig.

Oracle's Optimal Flexible Architecture

Optimal Flexible Architecture (OFA) is a directory structure created to assist the database administrator by keeping the many different files required to run Oracle software in predictable locations on disks.

Oracle touts many advantages to using OFA, but there are two advantages that are particularly important. First, implementing the OFA standard ensures that future administrators of the database will understand the file structure in place. This is a good reason to implement OFA using the exact directory names suggested by Oracle. Second, OFA makes adding new versions of Oracle software and switching between databases that use different versions of Oracle is possible and easy.

Figure 4.14 displays the OFA structure for an installation with two versions of Oracle software installed and two working databases. The databases are named db9i and db10g, suggesting that each database is running on a different software version.

On a typical production database server, there would be many mount-points. The disk mounted at /u01 is used to store the software versions. The database data-files of the various databases would be stored on disks mounted at /u02, /u03 and higher.

Oracle made a change to OFA with the release of Oracle 10g. Now, the $ORACLE_HOME for a 10g installation is kept in a sub-directory of 10.1.0. The sub-directory is called db_1. The reason for this change is that it allows for the install of the same product more than one time, such as creating a new 10g software install in the subdirectory db_2. It also allows for the install of a different Oracle product in a different sub-directory. For example, Oracle Client software could be installed in client_1.

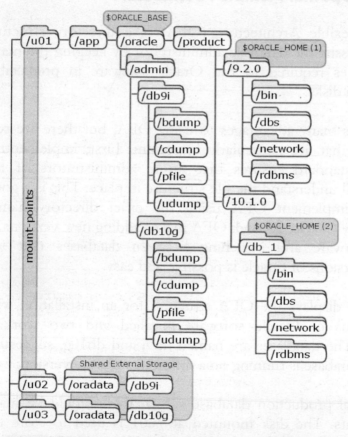

Figure 4.14: *Optimal flexible architecture file structure.*

To create the necessary directories for an Oracle 9i install, run the commands shown in Figure 4.15 on each node.

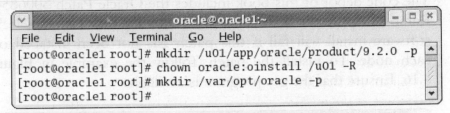

```
oracle@oracle1:~
File   Edit   View   Terminal   Go   Help
[root@oracle1 root]# mkdir /u01/app/oracle/product/9.2.0 -p
[root@oracle1 root]# chown oracle:oinstall /u01 -R
[root@oracle1 root]# mkdir /var/opt/oracle -p
[root@oracle1 root]#
```

Figure 4.15: *Making the necessary directories for an Oracle 9i install.*

Important Oracle Files outside of the OFA Directory Structure

There is small number of files that Oracle places in locations outside of the OFA directory structure. After an install, the files listed in the following table will be shown.

PATH AND FILE	DESCRIPTION
/etc/oratab (9i) /var/opt/oracle/oratab (user created link only - 10g)	The oratab file is used to identify each SID with its associated ORACLE_HOME.
/var/opt/oracle/srvConfig.loc (9i) /etc/oracle/ocr.loc (10g)	This is a text file that identifies the location of the file used for cluster configuration and srvctl repository.
/etc/oralnst.loc (9i & 10g)	Identifies the location on disk of the Oracle inventory files and identifies the OS user group that owns the Oracle install. For a 10g install, this file is located in the $ORACLE_HOME directory.
/usr/local/bin/oraenv /usr/local/bin/racenv /usr/local/bin/coraenv /usr/local/bin/dbhome	These scripts are used to set environmental variables. The oraenv and racenv scripts are Bash shell scripts used extensively in this book. The coraenv script is used in the C shell. The dbhome script is used by the other three scripts to identify the home directory associated with given database.

Table 4.5: *Files shown, after an install.*

Installing the Oracle Patch 3006854

The code depot of this book includes the Oracle Patch 3006854. Refer to Appendix B for download instructions. The Oracle 9i software install will fail if this patch has not been installed on each node. To install the patch, follow the example in Figure 4.16. Ensure that the gcc program is available.

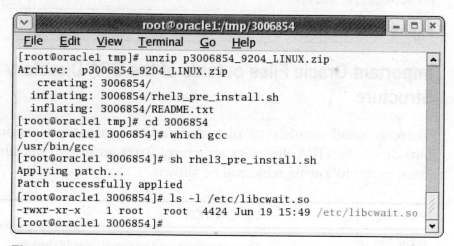

Figure 4.16: *Installing the Redhat Linux patch.*

If the patch failed, most system commands such as *ls* will now return an error, a major problem! Figure 4.17 demonstrates the error and what can be done to fix this error. The patch must still be successfully run so that the /etc/libcwait.so and /etc/ld.so.preload files exist on the file system.

Figure 4.17: *Run these commands only if the patch install failed.*

Conclusion

As this chapter has demonstrated, Linux is a highly configurable operating system, ideal for clustered Oracle servers. In the next chapter, we will continue our work by preparing the shared external disk drive for our install.

Configuring Shared Storage

A Real Application Cluster (RAC) database requires disk storage that can be accessed equally by all nodes within the cluster. This chapter will show how to configure the fire-wire drive used for the project in this book to meet that requirement. This chapter will demonstrate partitioning the drive so that it can be configured to act like the multiple disks available on a production server. It will also cover installing Oracle Cluster File System (OCFS) software on each node as well as formatting partitions on the shared drive.

Verifying the External Drive is Accessible to Each Node

The modified kernel that allows for dual logging on the external fire-wire drive has already been installed on each node. To ensure that the drive can be accessed, run the command fdisk -l /dev/sda from each node as shown in Figure 5.1. The prefix sd in /dev/sda is reserved for scsi drives. The new kernel detects the external drive as the first SCSI drive.

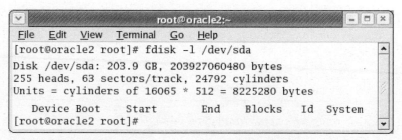

Figure 5.1: *Using fdisk to verify the external drive.*

Partitioning the External Drive

A change that is made by one node on the external drive can be read immediately by the other node. Therefore, the steps taken to partition the drive need only be done from one of the nodes.

A partition is a subdivision of the write space on a hard drive. A partition can be used to segregate different file systems. It can also be used to prevent one writing area from expanding and thus crowding out and overwriting other areas.

There are three types of partitions available: primary, extended and logical. There can be no more than four primary partitions on a single drive.

An extended partition works as a container in which to place logical partitions. Only one extended partition can be created on a drive, and an extended partition cannot be written to directly; it must be sub-divided by logical partitions.

The advantage to working with an extended partition and multiple logical partitions is that by combining the two, Linux can handle up to 15 partitions on one SCSI disk or 63 on an ide disk.

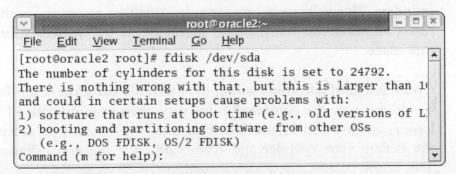

Figure 5.2: *Using fdisk to partition device /dev/sda.*

Use the fdisk utility to partition the external drive. Call it by using the command fdisk /dev/sda as shown in Figure 5.2. There are just a few commands that need to be remembered when using fdisk. These commands are: help (m), print a list of partitions (p), create a new partition (n), delete a partition (d), quit without saving (q), and write a new partition table and quit (w).

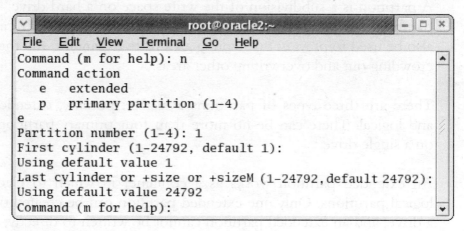

Figure 5.3: *Creating an extended partition.*

To create an extended partition, type the command n for new, then respond with e for extended as shown in Figure 5.3. Type [enter] to accept the default numbers for the first and last cylinders. This will create one extended partition across the entire drive, allowing for many logical partitions to be created within that space.

Creating logical partitions within the extended partition is simple. To do this type the command n for new, then respond with l for logical as shown in Figure 5.4. This time, type [enter] to accept the default start cylinder and type +20G for the end cylinder. This action creates a new logical partition of 20 gigabytes.

A 203 gigabyte drive was used to write this book. It was divided into 11 logical partitions; the first 10 partitions were sized at 20g and the last as a smaller left-over partition.

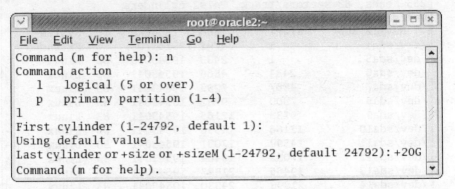

Figure 5.4: *Creating a logical partition.*

To complete all the exercises in this book, you will need the partitions configured with the following minimum sizes in mind:

PARTITIONS	WILL BE USED FOR	MINIMUM SIZE
sda5 through sda6	Oracle Cluster File System	10G each
sda7 through sda10	Raw	1G each
sda11 through sda14	Automatic Storage Management	10G each (all the same size)
sda15	extra partition	any size

Table 5.1: *Partitions configured with minimum sizes in mind*

Repeat the previous command 10 times to create 11 logical partitions. View the partitions with the command p for print. A printout of your partition table should look similar to the one in Figure 5.5. You will note that the first logical partition is associated with /dev/sda5 and that its first cylinder is 1, the same as the extended partition that contains the logical partitions.

```
┌─────────────────────────────────────────────────────────┐
│  ▼              root@oracle2:~            [_] [□] [x]     │
├─────────────────────────────────────────────────────────┤
│  File  Edit  View  Terminal  Go  Help                    │
├─────────────────────────────────────────────────────────┤
│ Command (m for help): p                              ▲   │
│ Disk /dev/sda: 203.9 GB, 203927060480 bytes              │
│ 255 heads, 63 sectors/track, 24792 cylinders             │
│ Units = cylinders of 16065 * 512 = 8225280 bytes         │
│    Device Boot    Start      End    Blocks   Id  System  │
│ /dev/sda1            1      24792 199141708+   5  Extended│
│ /dev/sda5            1       2433  19543009+  83  Linux   │
│ /dev/sda6         2434       4866  19543041   83  Linux   │
│ /dev/sda7         4867       7299  19543041   83  Linux   │
│ /dev/sda8         7300       9732  19543041   83  Linux   │
│ /dev/sda9         9733      12165  19543041   83  Linux   │
│ /dev/sda10       12166      14598  19543041   83  Linux   │
│ /dev/sda11       14599      17031  19543041   83  Linux   │
│ /dev/sda12       17032      19464  19543041   83  Linux   │
│ /dev/sda13       19465      21897  19543041   83  Linux   │
│ /dev/sda14       21898      24330  19543041   83  Linux   │
│ /dev/sda15       24331-     24792   3710983+  83  Linux   │
│ Command (m for help):                                ▼   │
└─────────────────────────────────────────────────────────┘
```

Figure 5.5: *Printing the partition table to the screen.*

Save the configuration by typing the command w which writes the new partition table to disk and exits fdisk. At this point it is possible to quit without saving by typing the q command.

The node, which did not write the partitions, needs to update the operating system to recognize the various partitions that were just created. Switch to the alternate node, login as root and type the command partprobe and then the command fdisk –l /dev/sda to list the partitions on the external drive. The list of partitions will match on both nodes.

Creating a File System

Linux supports many different file systems. A file system is a specific arrangement of disk data which allows the operating system to name and retrieve files from disk. A file system can contain file attributes which control the way a file or directory may be accessed. In Linux, these controls take the form of ownership and permissions to read from, write to and execute given files. The dates and times of creation and modification can also be maintained on a file system.

Although Linux can read from and write to many different file systems, the Fedora Core 1 distribution uses the ext3 file system by default. Ext3 is already being used on the internal hard disks of each node. This file system is a journaled file system which means that as files are written to disk, the file system maintains its own consistency. Journaling allows for speedy recovery in the event of an unclean shutdown; therefore, restarting after a sudden loss of power does not require a lengthy consistency check of the file system.

The ext3 file system cannot be used to store the shared files of a clustered database.

Oracle Cluster File System

Oracle has created a file system specifically tailored to the needs of RAC database files called Oracle Cluster File System or OCFS for short. OCFS must be downloaded and installed as a separate program from the Oracle database. OCFS maintains voting data among all of the nodes. This data is used to keep a consistent image of each file on disk to the different nodes of the cluster.

Raw - Storing Database Files without using a File System

Creating a partition without a file system, and reading and writing to this partition is referred to as using a raw partition or a raw device or simply raw. It is possible to create database files or even an entire database using raw. There are advantages to using raw partitions, such as I/O performance. And although the increase in I/O over OCFS is generally less than 5%, raw partitions move larger buffers of input and output than those moved by file systems.

Raw partitions are generally more difficult to administer than files on a file system. For example, only one file can be created on a raw partition and its path and name will be lost to the path and name of a device such as "/dev/raw/raw1." Symbolic links can be used to point to the device, providing a more meaningful path and name on the file system. The operating system commands that can normally be used to copy (cp) or move (mv) a file cannot be used on a file stored on a raw partition.

Automatic Storage Management

Oracle's Automatic Storage Management (ASM) combines advantages of raw partitions with the advantages of file systems. Instead of formatting and mounting a file system, ASM duplicates and balances file extents across multiple disk partitions without the need for the administrator to decide where to put them.

Although this technology was created to make administering I/O easier, the administrator cannot view files from the operating system, a concept that may take some getting used to. As you will see in Chapter 11, Release 2 of 10g software includes a command line tool that allows ASM files to respond to a limited set of commands as if they were on a standard file system.

Other File Systems used to Store Shared Database Files

There are other file systems which could be used to store Oracle database files in a RAC cluster. The Network File System is one which is supported by Linux. There are also a number of vendor specific Cluster File Systems available for different varieties of UNIX. However, they are not covered in this book.

Getting Started – Installing OCFS Software

The instructions for downloading and burning to disk all of the elements required to install OCFS can be found in Chapter 4. Review Chapter 4 and copy the files into the /tmp directory.

OCFS software must be installed as root using the rpm -ivh command. Do not login as another user and use the *su* command to install and configure OCFS! Make sure you login directly as root. There are four elements that need to be installed. Some of the files installed are dependent upon others, so install them in the order shown in Figure 5.6, and install the software on all nodes.

OCFS requires a version of modutils that is older than the one already installed with the Fedora kernel, so it must be forced in with the --force switch as shown in Figure 5.6. The necessary version of modutils is included in the code depot.

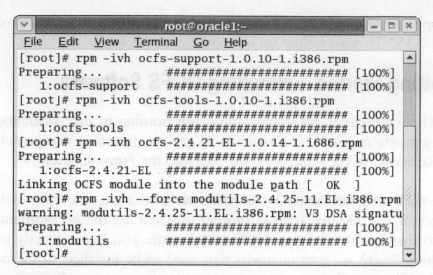

Figure 5.6: *Installing OCFS and Modutils.*

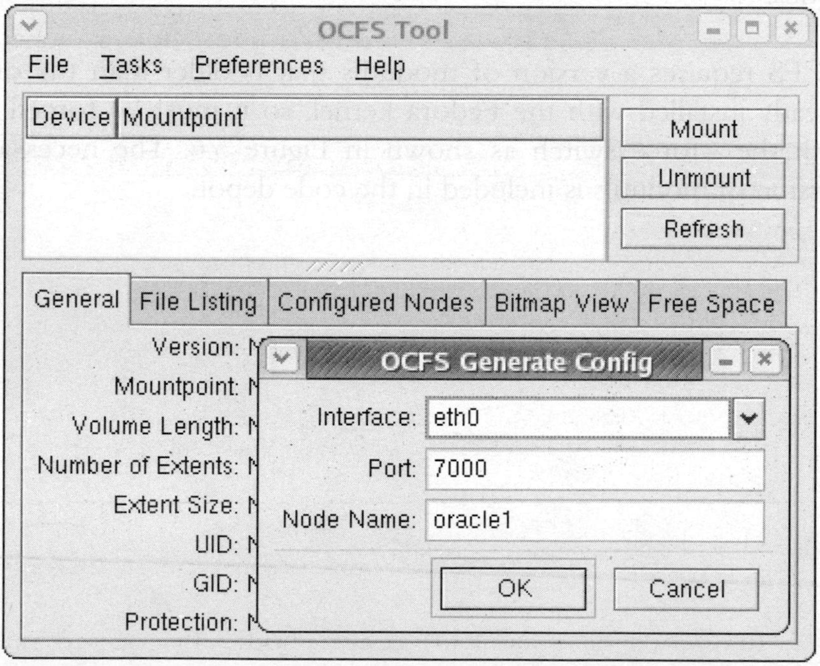

Figure 5.7: *Oracle Cluster File System Tool.*

Configuring OCFS

Once installed, OCFS can be configured by the root user. Launch the OCFS Tool with the command *ocfstool*. Click tasks, and then select generate config. As long as the network has been set up properly, the default values will be correct. This will create the text file /etc/ocfs.conf. Generate a configuration file and then quit the OCFS tool program. Viewing the configuration file is easy to do with the more command as seen in Figure 5.8. Finish this step on each node.

The parameter *comm_voting* = 1 tells OCFS to prefer the network to share voting information among the nodes. With this configuration if the network becomes unavailable, it will fail over to sharing voting information via the disk. If *comm_voting* = 0, voting information will be shared via the disk only. Using the network is preferred because it is faster and offers a fail-over option.

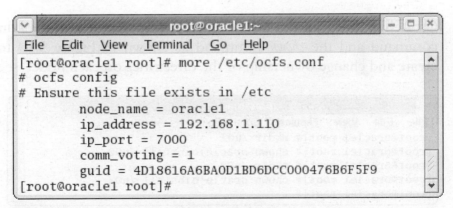

Figure 5.8: *Viewing the OCFS configuration.*

With the config file generated on each node, run the command *load_ocfs* on each node as shown in Figure 5.9.

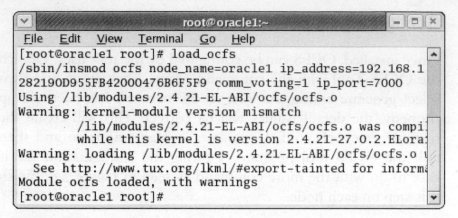

Figure 5.9: *load_ocfs*

The module will load with warnings. This is expected on Fedora Core 1. The *load_ocfs* command does not need to be run after rebooting because OCFS will be loaded automatically from the script /etc/init.d/ocfs, which was written to disk and turned on with chkconfig when OCFS was installed.

Create the directories to be used as mount points. Use the mkdir command and the *chown* command as shown in Figure 5.10 to create and change ownership of the directories on each node.

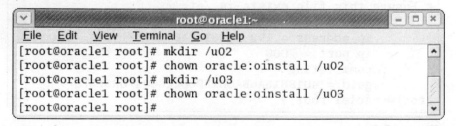

Figure 5.10: *Creating the mount-points for install.*

The directories /u02 and /u03 will be used to mount the shared partitions on the external drive.

Getting Started – Installing OCFS Software

With OCFS configured and loaded on each node in the cluster, *ocfstool* can now be used to format a partition on the shared firewire disk. Formatting a partition needs to be done from only one node. To do this, launch the OCFS tool again with the command *ocfstool*. Using the OCFS toolbar, choose Preferences and switch to Advanced as shown in Figure 5.11. This will add a few more options such as the force command.

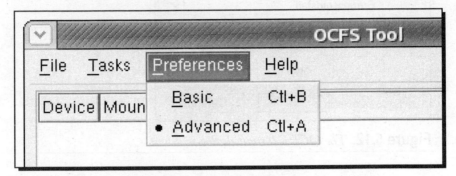

Figure 5.11: *Switching to advanced.*

From the toolbar, choose Tasks and then Format. A new window will appear as shown in Figure 5.12.

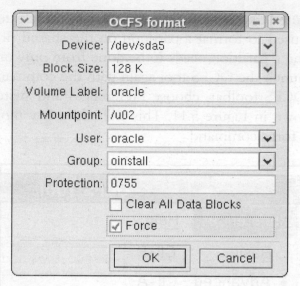

Figure 5.12: *The OCFS format dialog window.*

 Warning – when attempting to format a partition that has been previously formatted with OCFS, the formatter may get stuck, even if the force option is included. To overcome this problem, you can format the given partition with the ext3 file system using the command *mkfs -t ext3 /dev/sda5* (replacing sda5 with the partition in question). This will overwrite any header on that partition and subsequently allow the OCFS formatter to complete its task quickly. This is a valuable trick for starting from scratch on a previously used partition.

Use the settings shown in Figure 5.12 for the partition /dev/sda5, and use the mount-point /u03 for the partition /dev/sda6. The force option is useful when overwriting a pre-existing OCFS partition.

Mounting an OCFS Partition

Once the partitions are formatted, it is a simple matter to mount them using the OCFS Tool. Simply click on the partition you wish to mount and then click the mount button.

Mounting a partition from one node does not mount it from other nodes. Therefore, it is necessary to launch the OCFS Tool from each node and mount the OCFS partitions.

When rebooting, partitions do not mount by themselves. As discussed in Chapter 2, the configuration file /etc/fstab must be edited to include the devices that are mounted when a given node is booted. From each node, edit the /etc/fstab file to include the new entries as shown in Figure 5.13. The notation _netdev indicates that the device to be mounted requires the network devices to be started before mounting can take place.

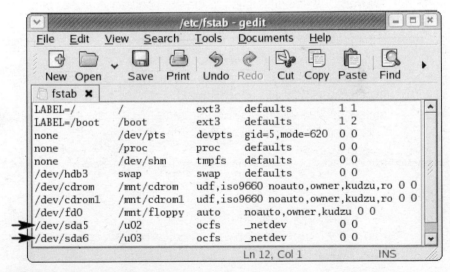

Figure 5.13: *Adding the new entries to the /etc/fstab configuration file.*

Conclusion

Preparing the external disk storage was the final step before actually installing Oracle software. Now, Chapter 6 will describe how to install Oracle 9i software for a RAC configuration.

Installing Oracle 9i Software

Pre-Work

Before beginning the installation of Oracle 9i software, verify that each of the following steps has been completed:

	CHECKLIST	
☑	Step to complete on each node	As described in
☐	Verify the required Linux packages have been installed by running the script *ensure_installed.sh* as root.	Chapter 2 and Appendix B
☐	The modified kernel should be installed and the file /etc/grub.conf should be configured.	Chapter 4
☐	Ensure the server parameters have been set by running the script *os_prep.sh* as root.	Chapter 4 and Appendix B
☐	Verify the Oracle user is created with a primary group of *oinstall* and secondary group of *dba*.	Chapter 4
☐	Ensure the Oracle user is able to use *rsh* to run commands from one node to the other.	Chapter 4
☐	Ensure the combination user:group "nobody" exists.	Chapter 4
☐	Ensure the file ~oracle/.bash_profile exports the correct default values.	Chapter 4
☐	Ensure the directory for $ORACLE_HOME is created and owned by oracle:*oinstall*. Ensure the /var/opt/oracle directory is created and owned by root:root.	Chapter 4
☐	Verify that Oracle patch 3006854 was properly installed. The ls –l /etc/libcwait.so command will list the file proving that the patch was applied.	Chapter 4 and Appendix B

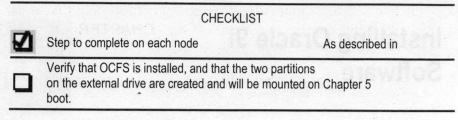

☑	Step to complete on each node	As described in
☐	Verify that OCFS is installed, and that the two partitions on the external drive are created and will be mounted on boot.	Chapter 5

Table 6.1: *Verify that each step has been completed*

Once the items in the checklist are verified, reboot each node to ensure stability. On boot, the nodes should be able to mount the external disks partitions. To ensure each node has done just that, login as oracle and issue the *df -h* command from each node to list the mounted partitions.

The first step when installing Oracle software is to set up two files on the shared storage. From one node, create the directory and files shown in Figure 6.1. The dd command is used to create binary files by reading from /dev/zero, a virtual device that outputs an unlimited supply of binary zeros.

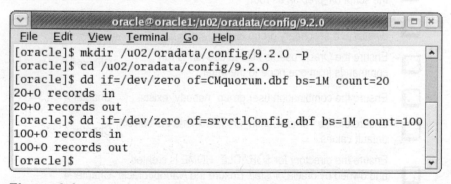

Figure 6.1: *Creating the shared configuration files.*

Verify that the files can be listed from each node. Figure 6.2 demonstrates the Oracle user listing the files from the node oracle2. These binary files will be used by the Cluster Manager and the srvctl programs to store configuration data that must be shared between the two nodes. Oracle 9i installation software requires these files and their directories be created in advance.

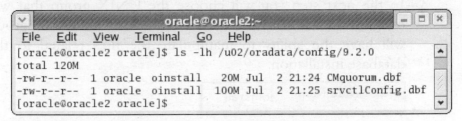

Figure 6.2: *Verifying the existence of the files from the alternate node.*

Installing Cluster Manager

Step-by-step instructions for installing Oracle Cluster Manager Software are detailed below.

1. Launch the Installer by inserting Disk One for Oracle 9i into the CDRom of the Oracle1 node. The operating system will mount the CD automatically and an icon for the CD will appear on the desktop. From a command line, launch the installer by typing the command /mnt/cdrom/runInstaller.

2. When the welcome screen appears, click next. If the environmental variable for $ORACLE_BASE is correct, the path for the base directory will appear as shown.

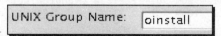

What would you like as the base directory?

`/u01/app/oracle/oraInventory`

3. In the next step you will choose the UNIX group that will own the Oracle software files. Members of the *oinstall* group will have the ability to manipulate the files related to the database installation.

UNIX Group Name: `oinstall`

4. To run the orainstRoot.sh script, open a new terminal window. Use the *su* command to switch to the root user, and then type the path and name of the script.

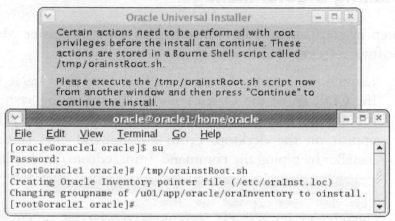

5. If the environmental variable $ORACLE_HOME is set, the destination path will be correct as shown above.

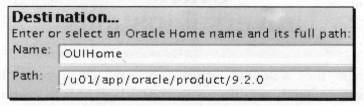

Destination...

Enter or select an Oracle Home name and its full path:

Name: `OUIHome`

Path: `/u01/app/oracle/product/9.2.0`

6. Choose the Oracle Cluster Manager software.

```
● Oracle Cluster Manager 9.2.0.4.0
  Oracle Cluster Manager, Release 9.2.0.4.0 for Linux Intel
```

7. Indicate the Public Node Names

```
Public Node 1:   oracle1

Public Node 2:   oracle2
```

8. Indicate the Private Node Names

```
Private Node 1:   int-oracle1

Private Node 2:   int-oracle2
```

9. Indicate the Quorum Disk Information (case sensitive!).

```
Quorum Disk Information   /u02/oradata/config/9.2.0/CMquorum.dbf
```

10. The summary screen will list the software that is about to be installed. As you watch the progression of the install, you will see that the files are copied from oracle1 to oracle2.

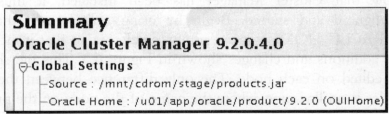

```
Summary
Oracle Cluster Manager 9.2.0.4.0
⊟ Global Settings
  ├ Source : /mnt/cdrom/stage/products.jar
  └ Oracle Home : /u01/app/oracle/product/9.2.0 (OUIHome)
```

11. The installation of Cluster Manager will finish quickly.

```
End of Installation
The installation of Oracle Cluster Manager was successful.
```

Configuring and Starting Cluster Manager

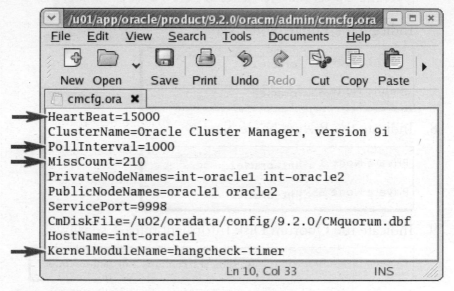

Figure 6.3: *Editing the cluster manager configuration file.*

Now that Cluster Manager has been installed, it must be configured and started. Begin by using *gedit* to edit the file $ORACLE_HOME/oracm/admin/cmcfg.ora so that it includes the additions and changes shown in Figure 6.3. This file should be edited on each node. The only difference between the two nodes is on line nine, where the name of the node on the private network is indicated.

To start the Cluster Manager, use the *su* command to switch to root user and issue the commands shown in Figure 6.4. Cluster Manager software relies on the hangcheck-timer kernel module which is preloaded with the parameters shown. The *ocmstart.sh* script starts the Oracle Cluster Manager software.

Use the command *ps –ef* to list all running processes. This command can be piped into *grep* which limits the output to lines

---

which contain *oracm* but do not contain *grep* as shown in Figure 6.4. It is normal for *oracm* to spawn several processes of itself.

```
oracle@oracle1:/home/oracle
File   Edit   View   Terminal   Go   Help
[oracle]$ su
Password:
[root]# /sbin/rmmod hangcheck-timer
rmmod: module hangcheck-timer is not loaded
[root]# /sbin/insmod hangcheck-timer hangcheck_tick=30 \
> hangcheck_margin=180
Using /lib/modules/2.4.21-27.0.2.ELorafw1/kernel/drivers/c
[root]# $ORACLE_HOME/oracm/bin/ocmstart.sh
oracm </dev/null 2>&1 >/u01/app/oracle/product/9.2.0/oracm
[root]# ps -ef | grep oracm | grep -v 'grep'
root     12276     1   0 11:14 pts/2    00:00:00 oracm
root     12278 12276   0 11:14 pts/2    00:00:00 oracm
root     12279 12278   0 11:14 pts/2    00:00:00 oracm
root     12280 12278   0 11:14 pts/2    00:00:00 oracm
root     12281 12278   0 11:14 pts/2    00:00:00 oracm
root     12282 12278   0 11:14 pts/2    00:00:00 oracm
root     12283 12278   0 11:14 pts/2    00:00:00 oracm
root     12284 12278   0 11:14 pts/2    00:00:00 oracm
root     12285 12278   0 11:14 pts/2    00:00:00 oracm
[root]#
```

Figure 6.4: *Starting the Oracle Cluster Manager as root.*

In order for the process *oracm* to run, the node it runs on must have read and write access to the shared configuration file CMquorum.dbf. If a problem is encountered, *oracm* will not be found by the *ps -ef* command. To find the problem, view the contents of the $ORACLE_HOME/oracm/log/cm.log file.

If it is necessary to stop the *oracm* process, use the *pkill oracm* command as root. In order to restart oracm, the file $ORACLE_HOME/oracm/log/ocmstart.ts must be deleted if its timestamp is too recent. It can be deleted with the rm command.

Installing Oracle Database Software

The following steps will guide you through the process necessary to install Oracle Software.

1. The installer CD 1 should be inserted into the CDRom on oracle1. Launch the oracle installer as the oracle user. Use the cd command to switch to the home directory of the oracle user, ensuring that the current working directory is not within the mount-point of the CD-Rom. It is important to be able to switch CDs! There should be no user with a current working directory as a subdirectory of the cdrom mount-point. Run the command /mnt/cdrom/runInstaller to launch the Universal Installer.

2. Hold the shift key and click the nodes to select them all. If all the nodes are not visible, then Cluster Manager is not running on all of them, in which case, quit the install and start Cluster Manager on each node.

3. If the $ORACLE_HOME variable is set properly, the path will be correct.

Destination...

Enter or select an Oracle Home name and its full path:

Name: OUIHome

Path: /u01/app/oracle/product/9.2.0

4. Select Database software for install.

> ⦿ Oracle9i Database 9.2.0.4.0
>   Installs an optional pre-configured starter database, prod
>   networking services, utilities and basic client software for

5. Choose Enterprise Edition.

> **What type of installation do you want?**
>
> ⦿ Enterprise Edition (2.84GB)
>
>   Provides data management for high-end applications such

6. Select Software Only.

> ⦿ Software Only
>   Installs software only and does not create a database at this time

7. The file named as the Shared Configuration File was pre-created on shared storage using the dd command. Type in the full path and filename (case sensitive!).

> Shared Configuration File Name /u02/oradata/config/9.2.0/srvctlConfig.dbf

8. The summary screen will list the software that is about to be installed.

> **Summary**
> **Oracle9i Database 9.2.0.4.0**
>
> ⊟ Global Settings
>   ├ Source : /mnt/cdrom/stage/products.jar
>   ├ Oracle Home : /u01/app/oracle/product/9.2.0 (OUIHome)
>   ├ Node Name : oracle1
>   ├ Node Name : oracle2
>   └ Installation Type : Enterprise Edition

9. To switch CDs, return to the terminal window from which *dbca* was launched. Press the [Enter] key to wake up the command prompt.

10. Unmount the cdrom with the *umount* command, and then eject it. Place the next CD into the CDRom and wait a moment for the system to mount it. Then, return to the Installer window and click the OK button to continue the install. This step will have to be repeated again in order to switch to CD 3.

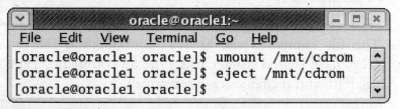

11. The installer will ask that a script be run as root. Open a new terminal window. Use the *su* command to switch to the root user and run the script. Accept the default value for the local bin directory by pressing [Enter]. Allow the script to finish on the first node before you begin it on the second. This step must be completed on each node.

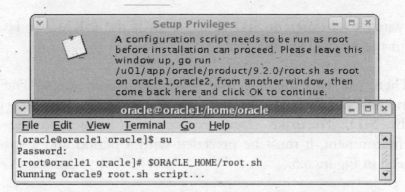

12. The entire software installation will require an hour or more on most systems. At the very end of the install, the Oracle Enterprise Manager will open for no apparent reason. Just quit the OEM.

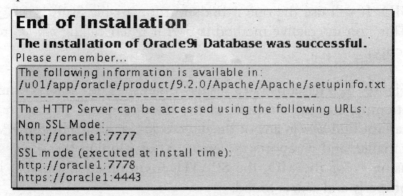

With the Oracle software installed, there are a number of tasks that must be completed before a RAC database can be created.

Setting Environmental Variables with oraenv

Oracle provides a script called oraenv that can be used to change the environmental variables $ORACLE_HOME, $ORACLE_SID, and $PATH to allow a user to connect to a given database instance (a database instance is often referred to as a "SID" or Oracle System Identifier). It can then be used again to switch to a different SID easily, even if the ORACLE_HOME for the new SID is different.

There are two methods for using the *oraenv* script. The first method is interactive, with the script asking the user to type in the SID. To make *oraenv* export the variables to the shell environment, it must be preceded with a period and a space as seen in Figure 6.5.

The second method for using *oraenv* is non-interactive. This is done by setting the variables $ORAENV_ASK=NO and $ORACLE_SID=<sid> and then running the script with a period and space before it. This time, *oraenv* will not ask for the SID. It will use the one it finds in the variable $ORACLE_SID. This non-interactive method is useful when calling *oraenv* from a script.

Figure 6.5 demonstrates using oraenv. The *which* command attempts to find the path to the *dbca* program. This command cannot find *dbca* in any of the directories identified by the $PATH variable, and it reports the error. After running the *oraenv* script using * for the SID, the $PATH environmental variable is set properly and *dbca* is found.

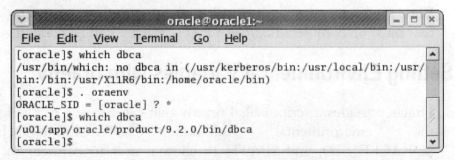

Figure 6.5: *Using the oraenv script to set environmental variables.*

Configuring and Starting the Listener on Each Node

A listener must be configured and running on each node in order to create a RAC database. The following is a list of steps taken when using the *netca* tool to configure and launch the listeners. This step needs to be done from only one node.

1. Use *oraenv* to set the $PATH and $ORACLE_HOME variables, then launch *netca*.

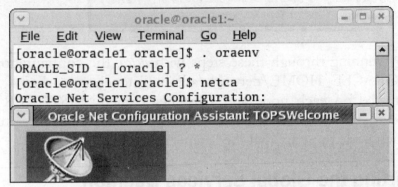

2. Choose cluster configuration.

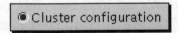

3. Select all of the nodes.

4. Add a listener.

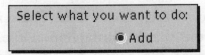

5. The listener name is LISTENER.

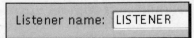

---

6. TCP is the only protocol needed.

7. Use port 1521.

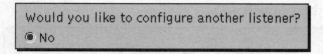

8. One listener is all that is needed.

Would you like to configure another listener?
◉ No

By running through these steps with *netca*, the configuration file $ORACLE_HOME/network/admin/listener.ora has been created on each node and a listener named "LISTENER" has been started on each node. Run the command *lsnrctl* status on each node to verify that the listener is started.

Starting the Global Services Daemon

The Oracle Enterprise Manager, *srvctl*, and *dbca* each rely on the Global Services Daemon service. *Srvctl* is a command line tool used to start and stop clustered databases (among other tasks as will be discussed in Chapter 7). Database Configuration Assistant cannot create a clustered database without the GSD service running on each node.

The universal installer has created the file /var/opt/oracle/srvConfig.loc on each node, which is a text file that defines the location of the shared configuration file. The universal installer has also issued the command srvconfig -init which initialized the shared configuration file. At this time, the Global Services Daemon (GSD) should start without error.

Figure 6.6 demonstrates the commands used to start the GSD service. Run these commands as Oracle on each node. If the GSD needs to be stopped, use the command *gsdctl* stop. The GSD keeps a log of requests made by the various clients of its service in the file $ORACLE_HOME/srvm/log/gsdaemon_<NodeName>.log

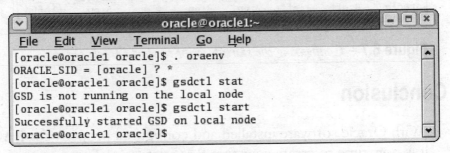

Figure 6.6: *Starting the gsd service for the first time.*

Ensuring Oracle Services Start on Boot

The code depot for this book includes a script called oracle that can be installed in the directory /etc/init.d. Once installed and configured to start on boot with the *chkconfig* command, the hangcheck-timer, *oracm*, *listener*, and *gsd* will start whenever the node boots. Switch to the root user and run the commands shown in Figure 6.7 to configure the oracle services to start at boot. This step must be completed on each node.

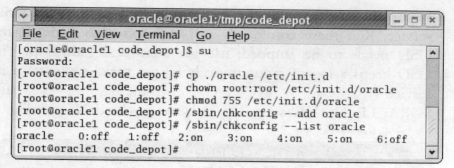

Figure 6.7 – *Configuring the startup script to start Oracle services.*

Conclusion

With Oracle software installed and configured properly for RAC, it is now time to create your first RAC database! The next chapter explains the steps taken to create and manage 9i RAC databases.

Creating and Managing 9i RAC Databases

Create a Basic Database

This chapter will cover creating a basic RAC database by using the *dbca* program. To save time, the author suggested that the first database created not include any optional features. This will cut database creation time down from hours to minutes. If a basic database can be created with the current configuration, then a database with more features can also be created.

The following documents the steps taken to build an Oracle 9i database.

1. Create all databases from the oracle1 node. To launch the Database Configuration Assistant (dbca), first set the $PATH environmental variable with . *oraenv*. Respond to the prompt with *. As the image suggests, there is a help file available with *dbca* that can be accessed with the command dbca -help. It is wise to be familiar with all of the switches available when launching dbca. In this case, run the database configuration assistant with the command dbca -datafileDestination /u02/oradata as shown.

2. If the option to create a clustered database is not available, Quit the *dbca* program then check that cluster manager and the global services daemon are running on each node.

3. Choose to create a database.

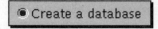

4. Select all of the nodes.

5. The new database template is useful to build a simple test database.

6. Name the first database created "test".

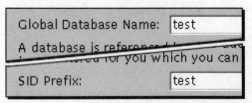

7. Database creation can take a very long time. If a simple database can be created with the current configuration, then any database can be created. To speed up the database

---

Create a Basic Database

creation, deselect all of the database options for the first database. When the dbca prompts to delete a tablespace, click "Yes". Click the "Standard Database Features" button to remove those features as well.

8. Choose dedicated server mode.

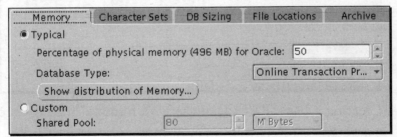

9. Any and all of these parameters can be changed after the database is created. Choose any configuration preferred, or simply use 50% of physical memory for Oracle.

10. The location of the spfile is indicated on the File Locations tab. It should have a path and file name as shown without having to edit it. If not, the -datafileDestination switch used to launch *dbca* was not correct. Upon clicking next, the *dbca* program will produce an error if the path for the *spfile* is not accessible by each node in the cluster.

---

11. Verify the path to each datafile by browsing through the items.

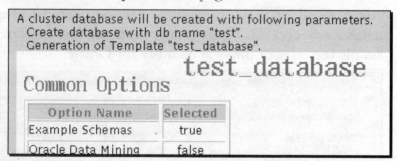

12. Ensure that the Create Database option is selected.

```
Select the following database creation options:
   ☑ Create Database
   ☐ Save as a Database Template
   Name:        [                    ]
   Description: [                    ]
```

13. Review the final parameters page.

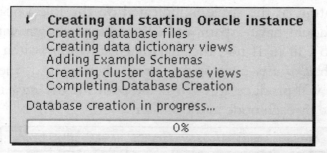

14. Creating a basic RAC database with minimal features requires about 30 minutes on most hardware.

```
 ✔  Creating and starting Oracle instance
     Creating database files
     Creating data dictionary views
     Adding Example Schemas
     Creating cluster database views
     Completing Database Creation

 Database creation in progress...

 [                    0%                    ]
```

15. Two errors are expected during database creation, depending on what features are included in the database. These errors can be ignored.

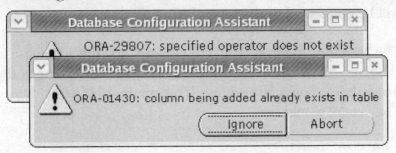

16. When the database is completed, fill change the passwords for SYS and SYSTEM.

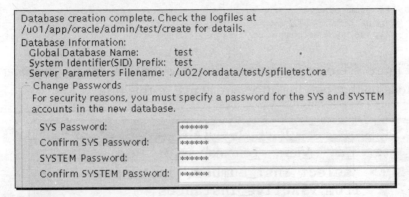

Using SQLPLUS

For many administrators, *sqlplus* will be the preferred tool to use to verify a new database's existence. There are two methods for connecting with *sqlplus*. The first method is to connect via the listener. The available syntaxes for a database named "test" would be:

```
$ sqlplus system@test/password
$ sqlplus system@test1/password
$ sqlplus system@test2/password
```

Using @test as the connect identifier, the listener will determine which instance to connect to. Using @test1, the listener will connect the user to the first instance, and using @test2 the user will be connected to the second instance.

The second method for connecting to the database is by exporting the variable $ORACLE_SID so that it names the SID that is hosted on a given node. This method bypasses the listener. The syntax would be:

```
$ ### from oracle1:
$ export ORACLE_SID=test1
$ sqlplus system/password

$ ### from oracle2:
$ export ORACLE_SID=test2
$ sqlplus system/password
```

Figure 7.1 demonstrates a simple query on *v$active_instances* that tells us that two instances are active at this time.

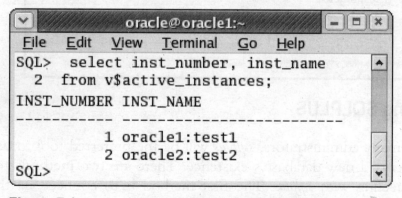

Figure 7.1: *Using sqlplus to verify the two instances*

GV$ Views

Most database administrators are familiar with *v$* views or dynamic performance views. A set of *gv$* views, or global dynamic performance views, has been created to support RAC

Create a Basic Database

databases. These views return information for all instances in a cluster. For example, *v$instance* will always return one row with information about the instance that is supporting the connection. On the other hand, *gv$instance* will return one row for each open instance in the cluster. For a list of these views, spool the query select *synonym_name* from *dba_synonyms* where *synonym_name* like 'GV%';

Some *gv$* views, such as *gv$instance*, *gv$session* and *gv$buffer_pool_statistics* are particularly useful for gathering system information across all instances. However, many *gv$* views return cartesian results. For example, *gv$active_instances* returns one row for each instance detected by each instance. So, if there are 3 instances in a cluster, you can expect 9 rows to be returned from this view.

racenv

The oraenv script is excellent for setting environmental variables, but it does not set the variable $ORACLE_SID with the additional numeric digit at the end. One option is to export the value for $ORACLE_SID by manually typing out the command. The code depot for this book includes the script racenv which can be used in the same way as the *oraenv* script but includes the numeric digit. Refer to Appendix B for installation and usage details.

Fixing Sqlplus and Other Command Line Tools

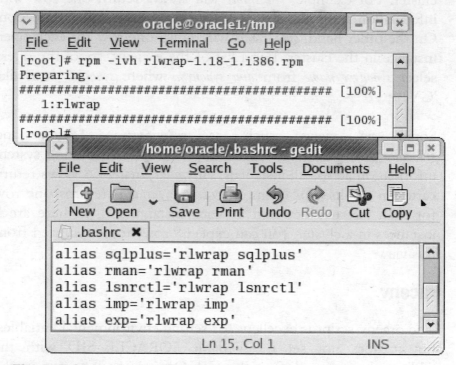

Figure 7.2: *Fixing command line tools with rlwrap*

If you have ever used *sqlplus* on a Microsoft Windows machine, you are aware that pressing the up arrow returns a history of the commands that were previously issued. This functionality was not included in the *sqlplus* for Linux, nor was it included in rman, *lsnrctl* or any of the other Oracle command line tools. To fix this, install the *rlwrap* program as root, then edit the file ~oracle/.bashrc to include the aliases shown in figure 7.2. To make the aliases effective, simply open a new gnome-terminal.

Using srvctl to Manage RAC Databases

A RAC database configuration requires extra tools to manage the software and instances. One such tool is *srvctl*, used to startup, shutdown and check the status a RAC database. A member of the Linux dba group can use this tool. *Sqlplus* can be used to start and stop an individual instance of a clustered database. *Srvctl*, on the other hand, can be used start or stop all the instances at once.

The following table shows the various uses for srvctl:

```
### Switches for srvctl:
# -d database_name    -i instance_name    -n node_name
# -o ORACLE_HOME (for add command)
# -o options (for startup and shutdown commands)

### Add a database or instance to srvctl repository:
srvctl add database -d test -o $ORACLE_HOME
srvctl add instance -d test -i test1 -n oracle1

### Remove a database or instance from srvctl repository:
srvctl remove instance -i test1
srvctl remove database -d test

### Print (to screen) the configuration of a database or instance:
srvctl config database -d test
srvctl config instance -i test1

### Modify the configuration of an instance to a different node:
srvctl modify  instance  -d test -i test1 -n new_oracle1

### Starting the database, all instances:
srvctl start database -d test

### Starting one instance:
srvctl start instance -d test -i test1

### Stopping a database, all instances:
srvctl stop database -d test
srvctl stop database -d test -o normal
srvctl stop database -d test -o transactional
srvctl stop database -d test -o immediate
srvctl stop database -d test -o abort

### Stopping one instance:
srvctl stop instance -d test -i test1 -o immediate

### Verify the status of the database, all instances:
srvctl status database -d test
```

```
### Verify the status of instance(s):
srvctl status instance -d test -i test1
srvctl status instance -d test -i test1,test2
```

Adding a Tablespace on a RAW partition

A raw partition (also known as a raw device) is a partition that has no file system and is not mounted, but it is still used to read and write data. Raw partitions were the first method for creating data files for RAC databases. They were used before OCFS was released.

Raw partitions are still in use and may be preferred by some administrators. Raw partitions are also a pre-cursor to Automatic Storage Management (ASM), which is Oracle's storage solution for 10g databases. It is possible to create an entire RAC database using raw partitions. For these reasons, it is important to understand the basics of raw partitions.

Even though the data files for the newly created database are stored on OCFS, it is a simple matter to add more tablespaces and store their associated data files on raw partitions.

To begin, verify that the raw devices /dev/raw/raw1 and /dev/raw/raw2 exist using the ls command to list them. Just as /dev/hda represents a hard disk, /dev/raw/raw1 is a device notation used to represent a raw device.

If the raw devices do not exist, issue the following commands as root to create them:

```
mkdir /dev/raw -p
mknod -m 660 /dev/raw/raw1 c 162 1
mknod -m 660 /dev/raw/raw2 c 162 2
```

Read the man page for *mknod* for more details on creating the block and character files used to control devices.

Create a Basic Database

To associate a device to an existing partition, switch to the root account and issue the commands shown in figure 7.3.

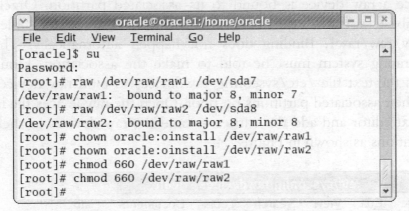

```
[oracle]$ su
Password:
[root]# raw /dev/raw/raw1 /dev/sda7
/dev/raw/raw1:  bound to major 8, minor 7
[root]# raw /dev/raw/raw2 /dev/sda8
/dev/raw/raw2:  bound to major 8, minor 8
[root]# chown oracle:oinstall /dev/raw/raw1
[root]# chown oracle:oinstall /dev/raw/raw2
[root]# chmod 660 /dev/raw/raw1
[root]# chmod 660 /dev/raw/raw2
[root]#
```

Figure 7.3: *Using the raw Command to Bind a Device to a Partition*

The raw command is used to inform the operating system that it must associate the raw device /dev/raw/raw1 to the partition /dev/sda9. This action is called binding a raw device to a partition. The *chown* command is used to change the ownership of the raw device to oracle:oinstall.

Commands used to manage files on a file system, such as *ls*, *cp*, *mv*, and *rm* cannot be used to manage a raw partition. The only operating system command that can be used to transfer data to and from a raw device is the dd command. It is possible to use the *dd* command to take a cold-backup of a raw partition database file, but it is more practical to use RMAN.

A raw partition can house only one contiguous chunk of data or "file." There are other limitations as well. For example, using the Logical Volume Manager, a limit of 255 partitions can be created and slated for raw "files" on a single physical disk. As an alternative to using a Logical Volume Manager, logical partitions can be used, as is demonstrated in these pages.

Once a raw device is bound to its associated partition, Oracle database software can read and write to the binary "file" /dev/raw/raw1. Binding does not happen automatically. The operating system must be told to make the association. Linux uses the text file /etc/sysconfig/rawdevices to bind raw devices to their associated partitions on boot. Open the rawdevices file in a text editor and add the entries to bind the raw devices to their partitions as shown in Figure 7.4.

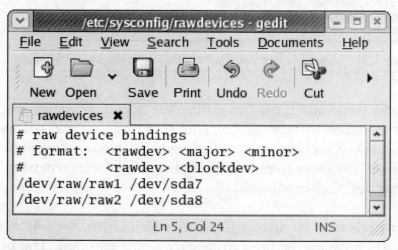

Figure 7.4: *Adding the Necessary Entries to /etc/sysconfig/rawdevices*

With the raw device bound to a partition, Oracle can use it for a tablespace. Create a tablespace with the command shown in Figure 7.5, and then create an additional tablespace using /dev/raw/raw2. It is important to use the REUSE keyword as Oracle will detect the raw partition as an existing file.

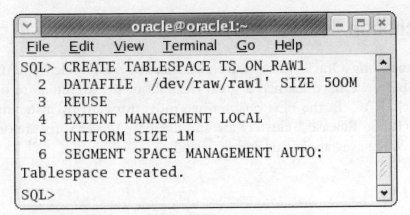

```
SQL> CREATE TABLESPACE TS_ON_RAW1
  2   DATAFILE '/dev/raw/raw1' SIZE 500M
  3   REUSE
  4   EXTENT MANAGEMENT LOCAL
  5   UNIFORM SIZE 1M
  6   SEGMENT SPACE MANAGEMENT AUTO;
Tablespace created.

SQL>
```

Figure 7.5: *Creating a Tablespace on /dev/raw/raw1*

An example of creating a table with 10,000 rows of data can be found in Figure 7.6. Use this example to create a few sample tables on the tablespaces you create. Having sample tables that you have created will enable you to validate upgrades as you continue with this project.

```
SQL> CREATE TABLE SAMPLE_TABLE (COL1 VARCHAR2(100))
  2    TABLESPACE TS_ON_RAW1;
Table created.
SQL> begin
  2     for x in 1..10000 loop
  3        insert into sample_table
  4           values (dbms_random.string('A',100));
  5        commit;
  6     end loop;
  7   end;
  8   /
PL/SQL procedure successfully completed.
SQL>
```

Figure 7.6: *Creating a Table with 10,000 Rows of Data*

Conclusion

By installing Oracle 9i software and creating an Oracle 9i RAC database, we have learned a great deal about the architecture of Oracle RAC. In the next chapter, we move forward by installing Oracle 10g Release 1 clusterware and database server software on the same hardware as our current install.

Installing Oracle 10g Release 1

Optimal Flexible Architecture and the Upgrade Install

With a working Oracle 9i RAC installation completed, the next step is to install the software for Oracle 10g release 1. It is important that the directories used for the install comply with the Optimal Flexible Architecture (OFA).

A problem arises with OFA in that the parent directories for the new clustering software, Cluster Ready Services (CRS), must be owned by root, and only root can have write access to those directories. In order to accomplish that task, the clustering software must be installed outside of the $ORACLE_BASE directory.

Figure 8.1 demonstrates the new $ORACLE_HOME for 10g and the $ORA_CRS_HOME for Cluster Ready Services, with root ownership of the parent directories.

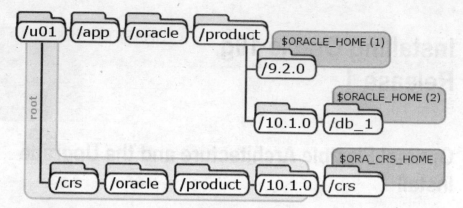

Figure 8.1: *OFA for a 9i and 10g RAC server.*

Although the name chosen for the home directory is a matter of personal preference, for this install, the home directory for CRS will be called crs instead of crs_1 because crs_1 could be misinterpreted to mean that more than one install of CRS is possible, which it is not.

Many database administrators will be happy to learn that 10g install software does not require directories to be pre-created.

Choosing RAW for Stability and Reliability

With an understanding of the administrative limitations of raw partitions, it may come as a surprise that for the CRS configuration and voting files, this book will use raw partitions instead of OCFS.

There are two very good reasons for doing so. The first is stability. Even after a successful install of CRS, with the configuration files on OCFS numerous instabilities have been seen. Rebooting tends to produce the error "INIT: Id hx respawning too fast" which indicates that one or more of the CRS services has failed.

The second reason is reliability of the install. Too frequently, when installing the CRS configuration files on OCFS, the error "PRIF-12: failed to initialize cluster support services" appears at the very end of the install.

Because of "interoperability problems with CRS and OCFS", the Metalink note 264699.1 recommends using raw partitions. The OCFS release notes list a bug #3467544 that states, "CSS fails to flush writes to voting file on OCFS."

What does Oracle recommend? – Two *different* articles found on Oracle's OTN website (http://otn.oracle.com) state that Oracle recommends using OCFS for the 10g CRS and voting files. These articles do not document where or why this recommendation was made. I have experienced enough difficulty to conclude that using raw to store these files, at least on this non-standard platform, is preferable.

Using a 9i srvconfig file stored on OCFS for the OCR file will consistently produces an error on a 10g upgrade install (Oracle bug #3940214). These problems may have been addressed with the release of OCFS version 1.0.11, but my experience would indicate otherwise.

Moving the srvctl Repository to Raw

In an upgrade install from 9i to 10g, the repository for srvctl is reused so that the configuration stored in it is not lost. At this moment, that file is stored on OCFS.

The following list provides walk-through steps for moving the current file to a raw partition and preparing a second raw partition for the 10g voting file:

---

1. As oracle, stop gsd on both nodes.

```
oracle@oracle1:~
File  Edit  View  Terminal  Go  Help
[oracle@oracle1 oracle]$ gsdctl stop
Successfully stopped GSD on local node
[oracle@oracle1 oracle]$
```

2. As root, bind the raw devices to the partitions as shown. Change ownership and permissions as shown. Repeat this step on each node. Raw3 will be used for the srvctl repository. Raw4 will be used for the 10g CRS voting file. The permissions on these files are critical to the success of the install!

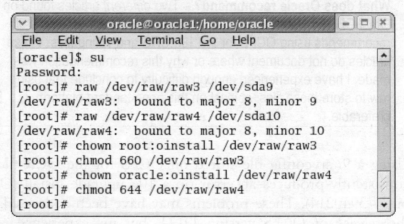

```
oracle@oracle1:/home/oracle
File  Edit  View  Terminal  Go  Help
[oracle]$ su
Password:
[root]# raw /dev/raw/raw3 /dev/sda9
/dev/raw/raw3:  bound to major 8, minor 9
[root]# raw /dev/raw/raw4 /dev/sda10
/dev/raw/raw4:  bound to major 8, minor 10
[root]# chown root:oinstall /dev/raw/raw3
[root]# chmod 660 /dev/raw/raw3
[root]# chown oracle:oinstall /dev/raw/raw4
[root]# chmod 644 /dev/raw/raw4
[root]#
```

3. As root, open the file /etc/sysconfig/rawdevices with a text editor and add the new raw partitions so they will be bound on reboot. Repeat this step on each node.

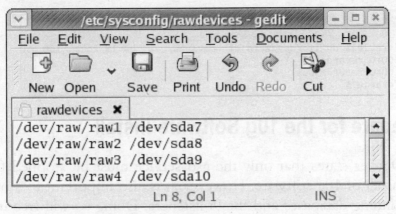

4. As root, open the file /var/opt/oracle/srvConfig.loc with a text editor and change the path to the raw partition as shown. Complete this step on each node.

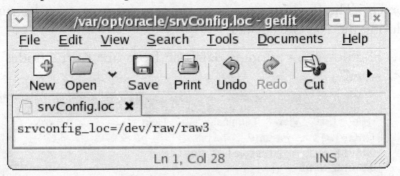

5. As oracle, start gsd on both nodes. This will ensure the file on the raw partition can be accessed properly.

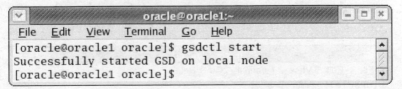

6. As oracle, use the dd command as shown to overwrite any stray data on the raw partition that will be used for the 10g voting file. This will help ensure a trouble free install. This step can be done from either one of the nodes.

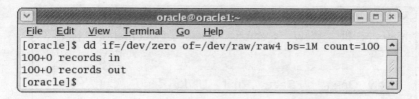

```
oracle@oracle1:~
File  Edit  View  Terminal  Go  Help
[oracle]$ dd if=/dev/zero of=/dev/raw/raw4 bs=1M count=100
100+0 records in
100+0 records out
[oracle]$
```

Prepare for the 10g Software Install

Oracles states that only the gsd service must be stopped for an install of 10g software. However, it is also important to stop any running databases and the 9i listeners. Doing so will free up the CPU, the RAM, and port 1521 for the 10g listener.

The following steps will stop all Oracle 9i services except the oracm. The 9i cluster manager process (oracm) must be running during the 10g CRS install.

1. Shutdown any running database from one of the nodes using srvctl.

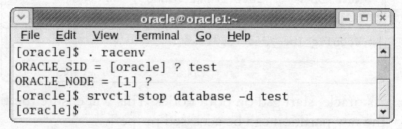

```
oracle@oracle1:~
File  Edit  View  Terminal  Go  Help
[oracle]$ . racenv
ORACLE_SID = [oracle] ? test
ORACLE_NODE = [1] ?
[oracle]$ srvctl stop database -d test
[oracle]$
```

2. Stop the gsd service and the listener. Complete this step on all nodes.

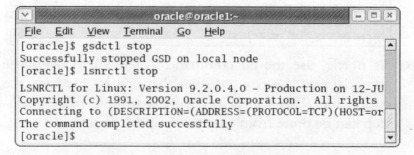

```
oracle@oracle1:~
File  Edit  View  Terminal  Go  Help
[oracle]$ gsdctl stop
Successfully stopped GSD on local node
[oracle]$ lsnrctl stop

LSNRCTL for Linux: Version 9.2.0.4.0 - Production on 12-JU
Copyright (c) 1991, 2002, Oracle Corporation.  All rights
Connecting to (DESCRIPTION=(ADDRESS=(PROTOCOL=TCP)(HOST=or
The command completed successfully
[oracle]$
```

3. As root, edit the file /etc/init.d/oracle so the ocmstart.sh script continues to start oracm on boot. It is necessary to hardcode the 9i ORACLE_HOME as shown. Comment out the lines that start the listener and gsd. These two services will be started and maintained by 10g Cluster Ready Services. Complete this step on all nodes.

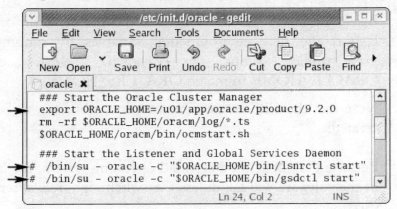

4. Next, use a text editor to edit the ~oracle/.bash_profile login script on all nodes so the default environmental variables are properly set for a 10g environment. Simply editing this file now will not update the variables for the current login. This will prepare for future logins.

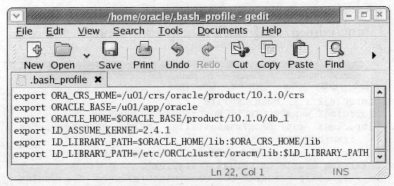

The 10g CRS Install

With the proper setup, the CRS install should complete easily. If an error is encountered, check Appendix C for a possible resolution. The following provides a walk through the steps of the install.

1. Insert the install CD for 10g CRS into the drive on oracle1. Export the new environmental variables by running the .bash_profile script as shown. Next, export ORACLE_HOME to match ORA_CRS_HOME.

   Note that the CRS home directory does not have to be pre-created!

   Because Fedora is not a certified operating system, the launch of the software will fail unless the switch –ignoreSysPrereqs is used.

   Oracle is trying to make the point that, as a company, they will not be supporting a version of Linux that does not meet their requirements. Fortunately, they have included this switch to get beyond the prerequisite check. Be sure to read through the available switches by running the /mnt/cdrom/runInstaller -help command.

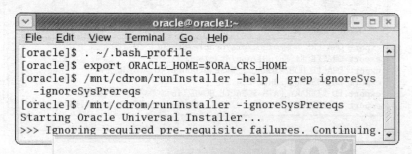

2. Verify the path to the crs directory is correct as shown.

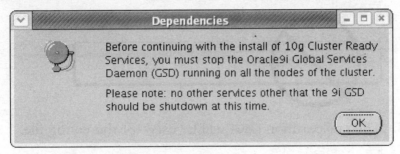

Destination
Enter or select a name for the installation and the full path
Na_me_: OUIHome1

P_ath_: /u01/crs/oracle/product/10.1.0/crs

3. Even though the gsd service was already stopped on both nodes, it is likely this warning will appear. Click OK and continue.

Dependencies

Before continuing with the install of 10g Cluster Ready Services, you must stop the Oracle9i Global Services Daemon (GSD) running on all the nodes of the cluster.

Please note: no other services other that the 9i GSD should be shutdown at this time.

OK

4. The default language "English" is available. Add any additional language(s) desired.

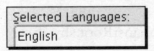

Selected Languages:
English

5. Indicate the public and private node names. The cluster name should be crs.

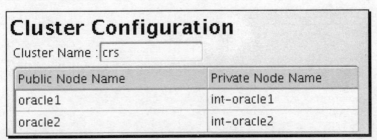

Cluster Configuration

Cluster Name : crs

Public Node Name	Private Node Name
oracle1	int-oracle1
oracle2	int-oracle2

6. Change the Interface Type by clicking on the rectangular area. This step identifies which network cards are being used for a given network.

Specify Network Interface Usage

Interface Name	Subnet	Interface Type
eth0	192.168.1.0	Private
eth1	192.168.2.0	Public ▼

7. When upgrading from 9i to 10g, this screen will not appear because the installer will verify the OCR file by reading the path and filename identified in the /var/opt/oracle/srvConfig.loc file.

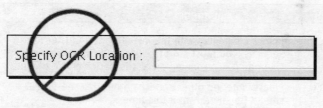

Specify OCR Location :

8. The raw partition raw4 will be used for the voting file.

Enter voting disk file name : /dev/raw/raw4

9. As root, run the script /u01/app/oracle/oraInventory/orainstRoot.sh from each node.

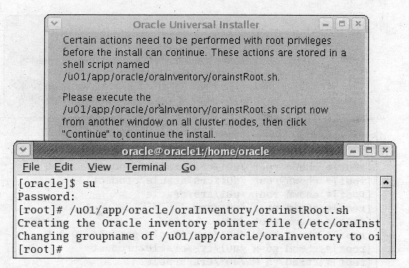

Certain actions need to be performed with root privileges before the install can continue. These actions are stored in a shell script named /u01/app/oracle/oraInventory/orainstRoot.sh.

Please execute the /u01/app/oracle/oraInventory/orainstRoot.sh script now from another window on all cluster nodes, then click "Continue" to continue the install.

```
oracle@oracle1:/home/oracle
File   Edit   View   Terminal   Go
[oracle]$ su
Password:
[root]# /u01/app/oracle/oraInventory/orainstRoot.sh
Creating the Oracle inventory pointer file (/etc/oraInst
Changing groupname of /u01/app/oracle/oraInventory to oi
[root]#
```

10. Review the summary of the install and proceed.

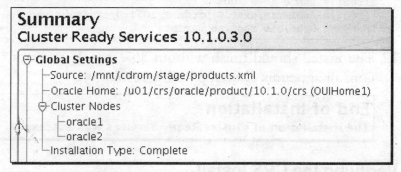

Summary
Cluster Ready Services 10.1.0.3.0

- Global Settings
  - Source: /mnt/cdrom/stage/products.xml
  - Oracle Home: /u01/crs/oracle/product/10.1.0/crs (OUIHome1)
  - Cluster Nodes
    - oracle1
    - oracle2
  - Installation Type: Complete

11. Before running the root.sh script, change ownership and permissions of the parent directories of crs. The chmod go-w command removes write access to group and others. Once ownership and permissions on these directories are changed, run the root.sh script. Allow the root.sh script to finish completely, then switch to the next node and run all of the same commands to complete this step.

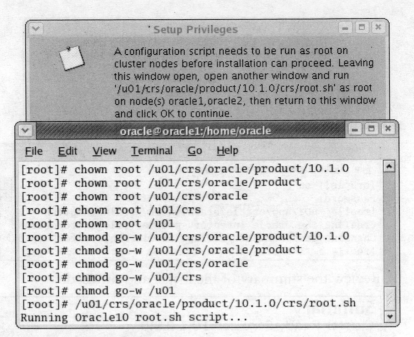

12. The install should finish without an error. If an error occurs, consult appendix C for a possible resolution.

End of Installation
The installation of Cluster Ready Services was successful.

Verifying the CRS Install

Oracle 10g CRS has installed three new daemons, namely evmd (Event Manager Daemon), cssd (Cluster Synchronization Services Daemon), and crsd (Cluster Ready Services Daemon). These three daemons should be running properly and should be spawned automatically on reboot. Use the command ps -ef | grep daemon_name to verify that a given daemon is running. This command should return many rows per daemon.

These daemons are not launched by a user created script like the "oracle" script used to start the 9i services. Instead, these daemons are launched by the init service. The /etc/inittab file configures the init service to respawn evmd or crsd if one fails. If cssd fails, the init service will reboot the node. Enter the command tail /etc/inittab -n3 as shown in Figure 8.2. The tail command will display the last three lines of the inittab file.

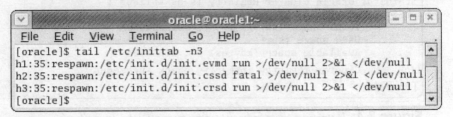

Figure 8.2: *The commands that launch CRS daemons.*

With 10g CRS installed, the pointer file used to identify the repository has changed. It used to be identified by the file /var/opt/oracle/srvConfig. Now, it is identified by the file /etc/oracle/ocr.loc. Figure 8.3 displays the text of these files. Note that the old file has been changed to point to /dev/null.

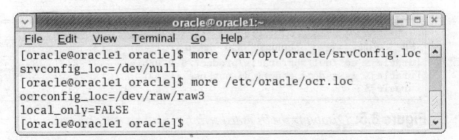

Figure 8.3: *Examine the contents of pointer files.*

Oracle provides the *ocrcheck* script to verify CRS has been installed properly. It should be run on both nodes as root. Figure 8.4 shows the typical output of that script. It is important that the version is "2" and that it states "integrity check succeeded" as shown.

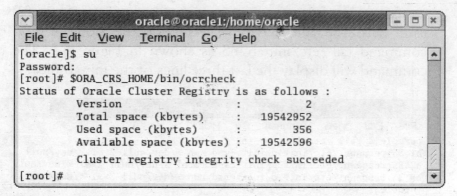

Figure 8.4: *Running the ocrcheck script to verify the install.*

The Global Services Daemon (gsd) is a service that supports both 9i and 10g software such as srvctl. The gsd must not be managed with the 9i version of gsdctl. Figure 8.5 displays the command used to rename the 9i version of gsdctl to ensure it will not be used by mistake. It is a good idea to rename this file on each node.

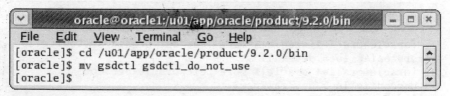

Figure 8.5: *Disabling the 9i gsdctl script.*

Installing Oracle 10g Database Software

CRS has been installed and verified. Now it is time to install the database software. The following information provides a walk-through of the steps of installation.

1. Start the install by unsetting the ORACLE_SID. In some cases, not doing so will cause an error. Run the *bash_profile* script as shown to export the environmental variables. As the image suggests, the runInstaller program has a help section

that should be read. Launch the installer with the −ignoreSysPrereqs switch.

2. Verify the path for the Oracle home. The 10g installer will create any necessary directories.

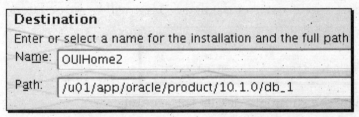

3. If the Cluster Installation screen does not appear as shown here, there is a problem with CRS, in which case quit the installer and debug. Otherwise, select all nodes and continue.

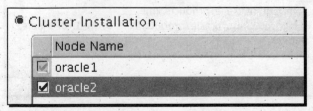

4. Select an Enterprise Edition install.

⦿ Enterprise Edition (877MB)

5. This system verify screen will appear briefly and then automatically move to the next screen. Do not click the back

button to return to this screen! Doing so will make it impossible to proceed further, requiring a relaunch of the installer.

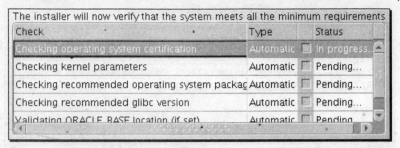

6. Do not upgrade an existing database. That will be done later.

7. Do not create a starter database. That will be done later.

8. Review the summary details for accuracy

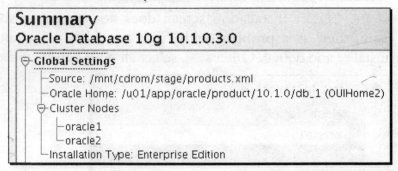

9. When the installer states it is copying files on remote node(s), be patient. It may appear nothing is happening, but it is simply a slow process.

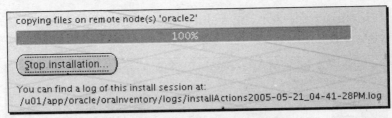

copying files on remote node(s) 'oracle2'

100%

Stop installation...

You can find a log of this install session at:
/u01/app/oracle/oraInventory/logs/installActions2005-05-21_04-41-28PM.log

10. As the script continues, answer "y" to overwrite the old versions of dbhome, oraenv, and coraenv.

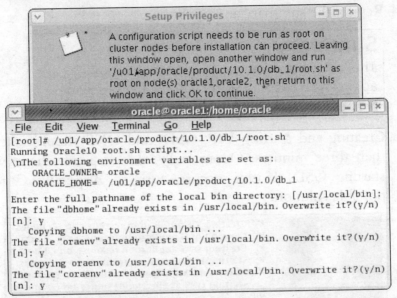

Setup Privileges

A configuration script needs to be run as root on cluster nodes before installation can proceed. Leaving this window open, open another window and run '/u01/app/oracle/product/10.1.0/db_1/root.sh' as root on node(s) oracle1,oracle2, then return to this window and click OK to continue.

oracle@oracle1:/home/oracle

File   Edit   View   Terminal   Go   Help

```
[root]# /u01/app/oracle/product/10.1.0/db_1/root.sh
Running Oracle10 root.sh script...
\nThe following environment variables are set as:
    ORACLE_OWNER= oracle
    ORACLE_HOME=  /u01/app/oracle/product/10.1.0/db_1
Enter the full pathname of the local bin directory: [/usr/local/bin]:
The file "dbhome" already exists in /usr/local/bin. Overwrite it?(y/n)
[n]: y
    Copying dbhome to /usr/local/bin ...
The file "oraenv" already exists in /usr/local/bin. Overwrite it?(y/n)
[n]: y
    Copying oraenv to /usr/local/bin ...
The file "coraenv" already exists in /usr/local/bin. Overwrite it?(y/n)
[n]: y
```

11. The VIP Configuration Assistant will automatically launch from the *root.sh* script.

> The VIP Configuration Assistant creates and configures VIP, GSD, and ONS resource applications for each cluster node.

12. Choose only the public ethernet card.

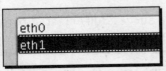

eth0
eth1

13. Populating the first "IP Alias Name" should automatically populate the remaining fields. If necessary, read the

---

/etc/hosts file for the values that were added there for the virtual IP's.

Node name	IP Alias Name	IP address	Subnet Mask
oracle1	vip-oracle1	192.168.2.151	255.255.255.0
oracle2	vip-oracle2	192.168.2.152	255.255.255.0

IP addresses are required for defining virtual IP resource application for each cluster node.

14. Review the summary and continue.

Summary
The VIP Configuration Assistant will now create application resources for each selected node.
Nodes: oracle1,oracle2

15. Creating and starting VIP, GSD, and ONS should take less than three minutes. Occasionally, this step may hang when starting GSD. If this occurs, turn to Appendix C for a possible solution.

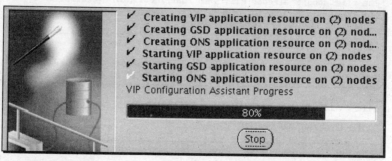

✔ Creating VIP application resource on (2) nodes
✔ Creating GSD application resource on (2) nod...
✔ Creating ONS application resource on (2) nod...
✔ Starting VIP application resource on (2) nodes
✔ Starting GSD application resource on (2) nodes
✔ Starting ONS application resource on (2) nodes
VIP Configuration Assistant Progress

80%

Stop

16. Review the configuration results and continue.

Configuration Results
The VIP Configuration Assistant has successfully created reso
Nodes: oracle1,oracle2

17. Don't forget to run the *root.sh* script from the other node(s).

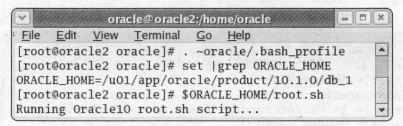

```
[root@oracle2 oracle]# . ~oracle/.bash_profile
[root@oracle2 oracle]# set |grep ORACLE_HOME
ORACLE_HOME=/u01/app/oracle/product/10.1.0/db_1
[root@oracle2 oracle]# $ORACLE_HOME/root.sh
Running Oracle10 root.sh script...
```

18. The installer reports the URLs of isqlplus and ultrasearch tools. All done!

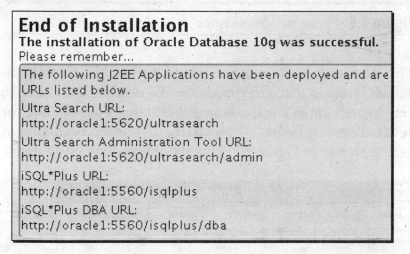

Post Installation - Fixing Scripts that Set Environmental Variables

The first step after an install is to fix a bug with the dbhome script. After the 10g install when the dbhome command is run, it will return the incorrect path for the $ORACLE_HOME of a given database. Fixing this is vital because the oraenv and racenv scripts rely on the dbhome script.

For some unknown reason, the 10g version of dbhome was written to look for the oratab file in the directory /var/opt/oracle. This problem is easily fixed. Simply create a symbolic link in that directory as shown in Figure 8.6. Do this on all nodes.

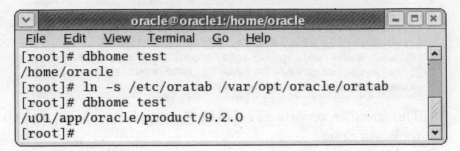

Figure 8.6: *Fixing the dbhome script.*

The next task is to remove the 9i ORACLE_HOME as the default home in the /etc/oratab file. To do this, as root, open the /etc/oratab file in a text editor and comment out the line for the 9i default oracle home "*" by placing a # at the beginning of the line, as shown in Figure 8.7. This should be done on all nodes.

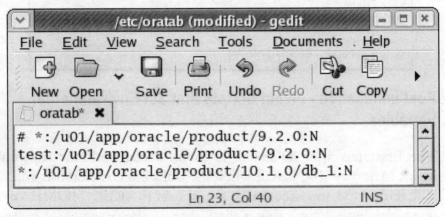

Figure 8.7: *Removing the default 9i Oralce home from /etc/oratab.*

Post Installation – Configuring the New Listener

Use the which command to ensure the netca to be used is the 10g version. If netca is not found, or if the 9i version is found, use oraenv to set the $PATH variable, then double check it with the which command. Launch the network configuration assistant from oracle1 with the netca command as shown in Figure 8.8. Choose "Cluster Configuration" to install the listener on all nodes and proceed by selecting all of the defaults.

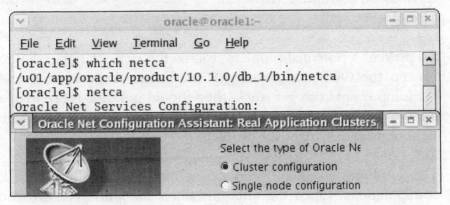

Figure 8.8: *Launching the 10g Network Configuration Assistant.*

Once the 10g listener is configured, forget about lsnrctl for starting and stopping the listener! The 10g Cluster Ready Services will be in charge of this service from this point forward. CRS considers the listener to be a critical service and will start it up after each boot. The listener will now be run as a process called LISTENER_<node_name> and can be verified with the ps –ef | grep LIS command.

The lsnrctl utility can be used to check the status of the listener with the command lsnrctl status LISTENER_<node_name>. However, attempting to start or stop the listener with lsnrctl will cause the lsnrctl program to hang. Using srvctl to start and stop the listener as a member of the nodeapps group is explained in Chapter 9.

Post Installation – Backing up the OCR

The OCR file for a 10g install contains far more configuration data than the srvctl repository from 9i. This file is far more likely to become corrupted, damaged, or mis-configured than in the case of a 9i install.

To prevent a potential problem, follow the steps in Figure 8.9 to backup the OCR and voting file. Although the ocrconfig and ocrdump scripts can get stuck, they should not take more than a minute to run. If they do get stuck, type [ctrl+C] to exit. Rebooting usually fixes the problem.

The ocrdump program produces a text file of all the OCR configurations. Open the after_install.txt file with gedit to read through the settings saved in the OCR repository.

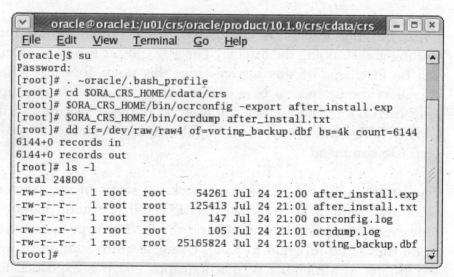

Figure 8.9: *Backing up the OCR file.*

Oracle CRS automatically takes a backup of the OCR file once every four hours. Unfortunately, the backup is taken after the first four hours, which is a good reason for exporting the OCR immediately after install. The periodic backups will be copied into the directory $ORA_CRS_HOME/cdata/<cluster_name[crs]> in the following format:

```
$ORA_CRS_HOME/cdata/crs/backup00.ocr   #( 4 hours old)
$ORA_CRS_HOME/cdata/crs/backup01.ocr   #( 8 hours old)
$ORA_CRS_HOME/cdata/crs/backup02.ocr   #(12 hours old)
$ORA_CRS_HOME/cdata/crs/day.ocr        #( 1 day   old)
$ORA_CRS_HOME/cdata/crs/week.ocr       #( 1 week  old)
```

After the install has been running for at least four hours, check both nodes for these files. You will likely find that these files are saved to only one node. The following is an example of restoring from the OCR from a saved backup:

```
### As root:
/etc/init.d/init.crs disable  # run on all nodes to disable crs
/etc/init.d/init.crs stop     # run on all to stop crs - allow 2-3
minutes!
cd $ORA_CRS_HOME/cdata/crs
dd if=/dev/zero of=/dev/raw/raw3 bs=1M count=100
$ORA_CRS_HOME/bin/ocrconfig -restore week.ocr
/etc/init.d/init.crs enable   # run on all nodes to enable crs
/sbin/init 6                  # run on all nodes to reboot
```

To restore from the export file after_install.exp, use the following commands:

```
### as root:
/etc/init.d/init.crs disable  # run on all nodes to disable crs
/etc/init.d/init.crs stop     # run on all to stop crs - allow 2-3
minutes!
cd $ORA_CRS_HOME/cdata/crs
dd if=/dev/zero of=/dev/raw/raw3 bs=1M count=100
$ORA_CRS_HOME/bin/ocrconfig -import after_install.exp
/etc/init.d/init.crs enable   # run on all nodes to enable crs
/sbin/init 6                  # run on all nodes to reboot
```

Understanding How CRS Manages the VIPs

VIPs are called "Virtual IPs" because they are not permanently assigned to a given NIC on a given node. A VIP could be supported by an alternate node in the cluster. To demonstrate this, the *crs_status* script needs to be installed. Verify this with the command which crs_status. If it is not installed, turn to appendix B for instructions.

With the *crs_status* script installed, shut down both nodes. Next, start up only oracle1 and login immediately. Quickly launch a gnome-terminal, and repeatedly run the crs_status command. This will allow you to view the progression of the crs services as they start, as shown in Figure 8.10.

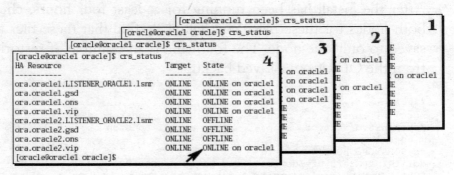

Figure 8.10: *Watching the progression of CRS services on startup.*

The vip is the first service to start. Client machines on the network are configured to find the listener at the vip address, so without it, crs will not start the listener.

After starting the vip, listener, gsd, and ons, oracle1 checks for the alternate node. With the alternate node absent, oracle1 starts the vip that is normally assigned to oracle2. Now, clients that are looking for a listener on oracle2 will find a node to connect to even though oracle2 is down.

Figure 8.11 demonstrates the use of the command /sbin/ifconfig | grep eth –A1 to view a list of IPs supported by the node and which NICs support them.

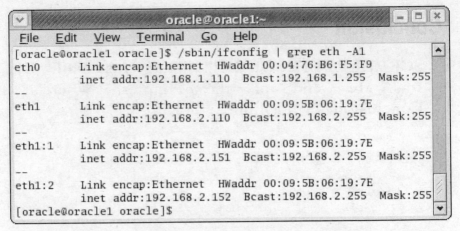

Figure 8.11: *Viewing which IPs are supported by which NICs.*

Now, start up oracle2. Allow it a few minutes to start up. Use the *crs_status* command repeatedly from oracle1 to watch the services of oracle2 come online. First, the vip is taken offline on oracle1. Then it is put online on oracle2. Figure 8.12 demonstrates the progression.

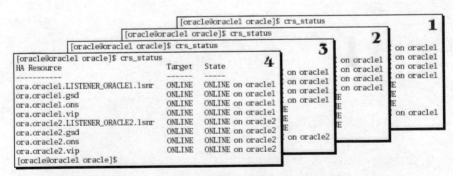

Figure 8.12: *From oracle1, watch the progression while oracle2 starts*

Conclusion

SCREEEEECH...OUCH!!! What was that!? Oh...it was the end of the chapter. Where's the Conclusion...Transition?

Creating and Managing 10g RAC Databases

Introduction

With the 10g software installed and the listeners configured, it is now easy to create a 10g database. 10g software is better prepared for the RAC environment than the 9i software. The Database Configuration Assistant has new features for creating databases in a RAC environment. One downside to the 10g software is that it requires more system resources such as cpu, ram and swap.

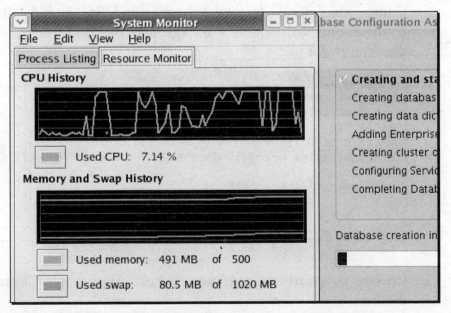

Figure 9.1: *Monitoring system activity during database creation.*

Gnome comes with a system monitor that can be very useful when creating a 10g database. Having it open during database creation will help determine if the system is hanging, which can happen when using old computers.

Launch the system monitor with the command gnome-system-monitor or find the monitor in the Redhat launcher menu. If the CPU activity stays near zero for more than a few seconds, the system is hanging.

Creating a 10g Database on OCFS

The following walks through the steps for creating a 10g RAC database.

1. Use *oraenv* or *racenv* to set the environmental variables and launch the dbca. Use the ampersand to launch the configuration assistant as a background process, freeing up the prompt for use.

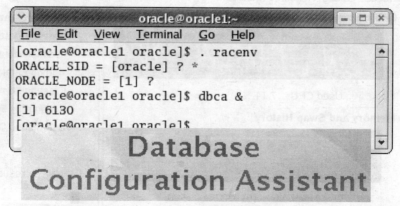

2. Choose to create or configure a Real Application Cluster database.

3. Choose to Create a Database.

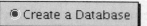

4. Ensure that all nodes are selected.

5. Select Custom Database.

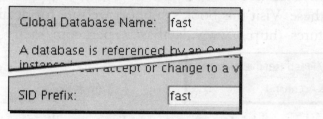

6. Use any name you wish except that of a pre-existing database.

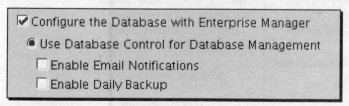

7. If you choose to configure a database with Enterprise Manager, be aware that doing so will launch the emwd.ps daemon. This will allow you to manage the database from a browser on a remote computer. Take note of the URL displayed on the "Database creation complete" screen at the end of the install.

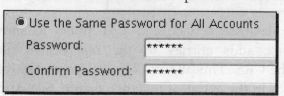

8. It is easier to use the same password for all accounts.

9. This new feature is a big improvement over the 9i version of dbca. Choose Cluster File System and continue.

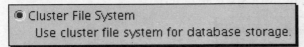

10. Indicate a directory on shared storage as shown.

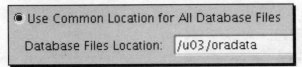

11. This book does not cover Flash Recovery or Archiving so deselect these. Visit this book's support website for details on these features. (http://www.database-expert.com/rac).

12. To save time on database creation, eliminate all unnecessary options as shown. If you chose to configure the database with Enterprise Manager, then leave the checkbox for the EM repository checked.

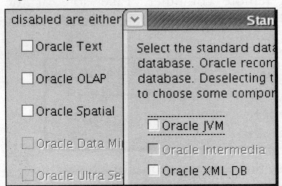

13. Configure the database service and TAF policy as shown. A database service adds entries to the *tnsnames.ora* file and resources to the CRS. This allows connections to failover to a backup instance in the event of instance failure. See Appendix

H for more information about database services for high availability.

14. This is simply a warning; do not configure memory usage below 44%.

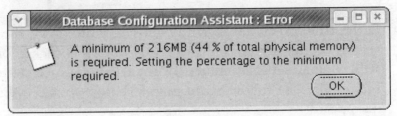

15. Depending on the available RAM, 60% memory allocation is a good start.

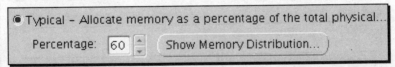

16. Verify the file locations for the datafiles.

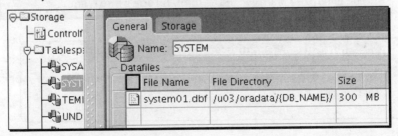

17. Choose to Create Database.

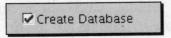

18. Review the parameters before the last OK button is clicked.

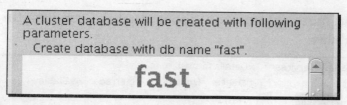

A cluster database will be created with following parameters.

Create database with db name "fast".

fast

19. If the options were not included, database creation will take about an hour. If an error occurs, it will almost certainly happen in the first minute or two.

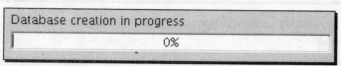

Database creation in progress

0%

20. If the Enterprise Manager was chosen, write down the URL shown on this screen. Once the OK button is clicked on this screen, allow several minutes for the database to be started on each node. The following message will pop up and eventually disappear.

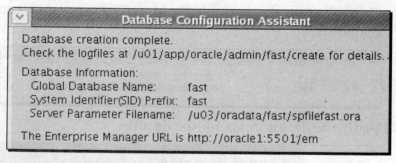

Database Configuration Assistant

Database creation complete.
Check the logfiles at /u01/app/oracle/admin/fast/create for details.

Database Information:
  Global Database Name: fast
  System Identifier(SID) Prefix: fast
  Server Parameter Filename: /u03/oradata/fast/spfilefast.ora

The Enterprise Manager URL is http://oracle1:5501/em

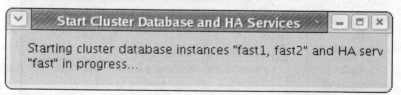

Start Cluster Database and HA Services

Starting cluster database instances "fast1, fast2" and HA serv "fast" in progress...

The Oracle 10g RAC database configuration is far different from the 9i database configuration. By default, CRS will attempt to keep everything, including databases, running at all times. If

---

nodes are rebooted at this time, the instances will be restarted automatically.

Check the status of services with the *crs_status* command as shown in Figure 9.2. 10g databases will be listed in the output of this command. However 9i databases, even when registered in the CRS, will not.

```
oracle@oracle1:~
File   Edit   View   Terminal   Go   Help
[oracle]$ crs_status
HA Resource                          Target      State
-----------                          ------      -----
ora.fast.db                          ONLINE      ONLINE on oracle1
ora.fast.fast1.inst                  ONLINE      ONLINE on oracle1
ora.fast.fast2.inst                  ONLINE      ONLINE on oracle2
ora.fast.fast_conn.cs                ONLINE      ONLINE on oracle1
ora.fast.fast_conn.fast1.srv         ONLINE      ONLINE on oracle1
ora.fast.fast_conn.fast2.srv         ONLINE      ONLINE on oracle2
ora.oracle1.LISTENER_ORACLE1.lsnr    ONLINE      ONLINE on oracle1
ora.oracle1.gsd                      ONLINE      ONLINE on oracle1
ora.oracle1.ons                      ONLINE      ONLINE on oracle1
ora.oracle1.vip                      ONLINE      ONLINE on oracle1
ora.oracle2.LISTENER_ORACLE2.lsnr    ONLINE      ONLINE on oracle2
ora.oracle2.gsd                      ONLINE      ONLINE on oracle2
ora.oracle2.ons                      ONLINE      ONLINE on oracle2
ora.oracle2.vip                      ONLINE      ONLINE on oracle2
[oracle]$
```

Figure 9.2: *Checking the status of services controlled by CRS.*

What are these additional resources in the CRS that end with ".cs" and ".srv"? These are the resources for the database high availability service that were created. The following commands can be used to read each service's complete configuration, including Oracle's description.

```
$ORA_CRS_HOME/bin/crs_stat -p ora.fast.fast_conn.cs
$ORA_CRS_HOME/bin/crs_stat -p ora.fast.fast_conn.fast1.srv
$ORA_CRS_HOME/bin/crs_stat -p ora.fast.fast_conn.fast2.srv
```

Turn to Appendix H for more information about configuring database services for high availability.

10g srvctl

With the new Cluster Ready Services added to Oracle 10g software, a number of new commands are available. For example, the srvctl utility is now used to start, stop and check the status of vip, gsd, listener, and ons as a group. This group of programs is referred to as "nodeapps." Figure 9.3 demonstrates checking the status of nodeapps.

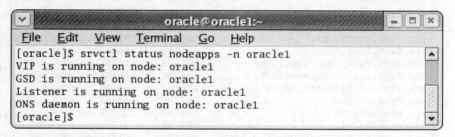

Figure 9.3: *Verify the status of nodeapps.*

A few new verbs have been added to srvctl's vocabulary. The following table provides some examples:

```
### Disable a database so that it does not start on boot:
srvctl stop database -d mydb
srvctl disable database -d mydb

### Enable a database:
srvctl enable database -d mydb

### Make an instance dependent on another service
### (mydb will not be started until +ASM service is running)
srvctl modify instance -d mydb -i mydb1 -s +ASM1
srvctl modify instance -d mydb -i mydb2 -s +ASM2
```

For a more complete list of new srvctl functionalities, visit the website http://tahiti.oracle.com to find the Oracle Real Application Clusters Administrator's Guide (Part Number

B10765-02), and look for the subheading "B Server Control (SRVCTL) Reference."

CRS Utilities

A number of CRS utilities, as listed in Figure 9.4, are included with 10g Cluster Ready Services. Looking at the help available for each of these programs through the command and the tag –help, demonstrates that most of these programs can do many things.

Unfortunately, these programs are poorly documented by Oracle. What you should know about them is that they can be used to add 3rd party applications to a cluster for fault tolerance.

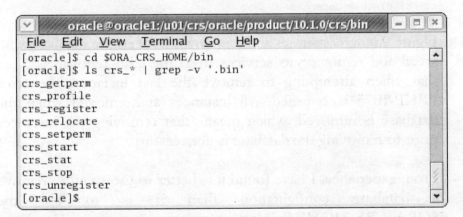

```
oracle@oracle1:/u01/crs/oracle/product/10.1.0/crs/bin
File   Edit   View   Terminal   Go   Help
[oracle]$ cd $ORA_CRS_HOME/bin
[oracle]$ ls crs_* | grep -v '.bin'
crs_getperm
crs_profile
crs_register
crs_relocate
crs_setperm
crs_start
crs_stat
crs_stop
crs_unregister
[oracle]$
```

Figure 9.4: *Listing CRS utilities.*

Figure 9.5 demonstrates using the *crs_start* script to start a database service after it has been shutdown by srvctl. Even though the response from the program only mentions member 'oracle1', the database is started on both nodes. This is only shown as a demonstration; I suggest using srvctl to start and stop databases.

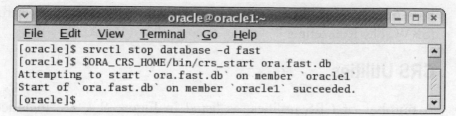

```
oracle@oracle1:~
File  Edit  View  Terminal  Go  Help
[oracle]$ srvctl stop database -d fast
[oracle]$ $ORA_CRS_HOME/bin/crs_start ora.fast.db
Attempting to start `ora.fast.db` on member `oracle1`
Start of `ora.fast.db` on member `oracle1` succeeded.
[oracle]$
```

Figure 9.5: *Starting a database dervice with crs_start.*

Before building the next database, it is a good idea to shutdown the existing database and to prevent it from restarting. Use srvctl to disable the database with the following commands:

```
srvctl stop database -d fast
srvctl disable database -d fast
```

Figure 9.6 demonstrates shutting down the existing database with srvctl and removing its services from the CRS repository. Note that when attempting to remove the last instance, the error PRKP-1075 is returned. All instances are removed when the database is removed, which means that removing the instances prior to removing the database is unnecessary.

From experience, I have found it is better to use srvctl to remove a database configuration than it is to use the $ORA_CRS_HOME/bin/crs_unregister command. The latter command leaves too much of the configuration orphaned in the CRS file, making it impossible to add a database with the same name back in later. However, crs_unregister can be used to clean up any orphan configuration that srvctl missed. An example can be found in Appendix C.

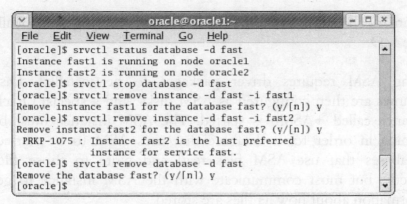

Figure 9.6: *Shutting down existing database and removing it from CRS.*

Automatic Storage Management

Having created both 9i and 10g RAC databases using OCFS, it is time to take a look at Automatic Storage Management or ASM.

Internally, ASM is very similar to RAW. 10g release 1 does not provide for a file system method for listing, moving or copying files stored on ASM. Instead, the administrator must use database views such as *dba_data_files* or *v$datafile* to list the files and rman to back them up.

Despite these apparent shortfalls, ASM offers many advantages. For example, ASM makes it very easy to configure redundant disk volumes. This means that if a physical disk fails, no database with ASM files stored on that disk will go down.

Replacing the failed disk drive is a simple matter. The disk can be hot-swapped, configured as an ASM volume and added to the disk group. At that point, ASM will automatically rebalance the database files stored within the disk group.

ASM optimizes I/O performance by automatically dividing files into extents and distributing those extents across available volumes. The administrator is thus freed from having to manually tune I/O.

Using ASM requires driver packages to be installed. Disk volumes are then configured as ASM disks, and a special Oracle instance called +ASMn is started. The ASM instance must be running in order for a database that uses ASM to be started. Databases that use ASM files read and write to those files directly, but must communicate with the ASM instance to get information about how its files are stored.

The ASM instance has two background processes new to 10g, namely RBAL and ARBn. These processes work together to rebalance extents across the disks. ARBn is spawned when the ASM instance requires it.

A database that stores data on ASM volumes has two new background processes; RBAL and ASMB. RBAL performs global opens of the disks. ASMB connects to the +ASMn instance to communicate information such as file creation and deletion.

The following table walks through the steps for installing the ASM drivers:

1. As root, install the three ASM driver packages in the order shown. This step must be completed on each node.

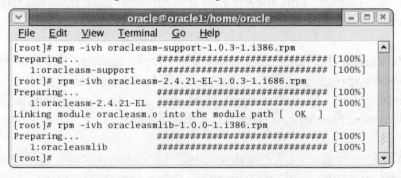

2. As root, configure the ASM driver to be owned by oracle:oinstall and start ASM on boot as shown above. This step must be completed on each node.

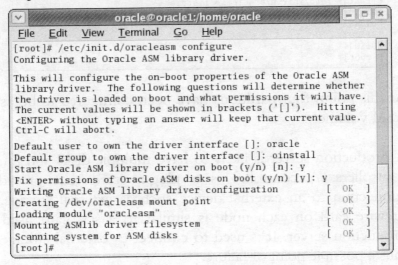

```
oracle@oracle1:/home/oracle

File   Edit   View   Terminal   Go   Help
[root]# /etc/init.d/oracleasm configure
Configuring the Oracle ASM library driver.

This will configure the on-boot properties of the Oracle ASM
library driver.  The following questions will determine whether
the driver is loaded on boot and what permissions it will have.
The current values will be shown in brackets ('[]').  Hitting
<ENTER> without typing an answer will keep that current value.
Ctrl-C will abort.

Default user to own the driver interface []: oracle
Default group to own the driver interface []: oinstall
Start Oracle ASM library driver on boot (y/n) [n]: y
Fix permissions of Oracle ASM disks on boot (y/n) [y]: y
Writing Oracle ASM library driver configuration        [  OK  ]
Creating /dev/oracleasm mount point                    [  OK  ]
Loading module "oracleasm"                             [  OK  ]
Mounting ASMlib driver filesystem                      [  OK  ]
Scanning system for ASM disks                          [  OK  ]
[root]#
```

3. As root, from oracle1, create ASM volumes on four unused partitions of the shared drive as shown. This step writes a header to each volume identifying it as an ASM volume.

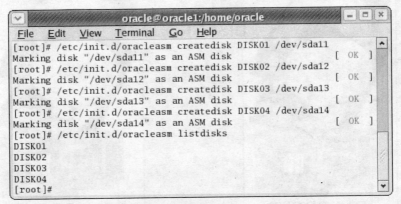

```
oracle@oracle1:/home/oracle

File   Edit   View   Terminal   Go   Help
[root]# /etc/init.d/oracleasm createdisk DISK01 /dev/sda11
Marking disk "/dev/sda11" as an ASM disk                [  OK  ]
[root]# /etc/init.d/oracleasm createdisk DISK02 /dev/sda12
Marking disk "/dev/sda12" as an ASM disk                [  OK  ]
[root]# /etc/init.d/oracleasm createdisk DISK03 /dev/sda13
Marking disk "/dev/sda13" as an ASM disk                [  OK  ]
[root]# /etc/init.d/oracleasm createdisk DISK04 /dev/sda14
Marking disk "/dev/sda14" as an ASM disk                [  OK  ]
[root]# /etc/init.d/oracleasm listdisks
DISK01
DISK02
DISK03
DISK04
[root]#
```

4. As root, from oracle2, scan the existing partitions for ASM volumes. This will detect the volumes created from oracle1 in the previous step

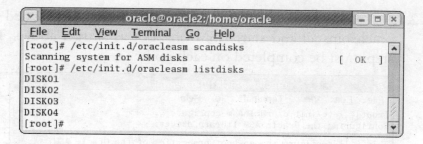

```
[root]# /etc/init.d/oracleasm scandisks
Scanning system for ASM disks              [  OK  ]
[root]# /etc/init.d/oracleasm listdisks
DISK01
DISK02
DISK03
DISK04
[root]#
```

At this point, four partitions have been configured to be used as ASM volumes.

A production server is likely to have multiple disks and multiple controllers. A controller is a plug-in card that provides a connection to an external device such as external storage. The firewire card on each node is similar to a scsi card used in a production server. It is used to connect to external storage, and thus a possible point of failure.

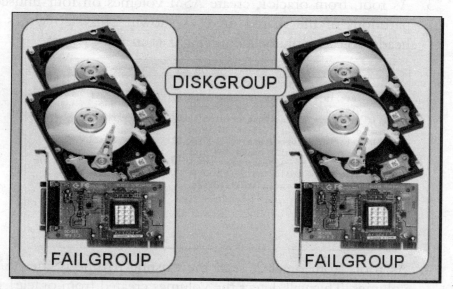

Figure 9.7: *A single diskgroup made up of two failgroups.*

Because a controller is a possible point of failure, Oracle provides a way of subdividing an ASM diskgroup into failgroups. Figure 9.7 shows how a server with two pairs of external disks attached to separate controllers is configured as a single diskgroup made up of two failgroups.

Although our hardware is not the same, for the sake of this exercise, we will mimic this configuration by assuming ASM volumes DISK01 and DISK02 are separate disks on a single controller, and volumes DISK03 and DISK04 are separate disks on a different controller. By doing so, ASM will mirror extents on each failgroup, ensuring that databases stay up even if a controller were to fail.

It is possible to use dbca to create an ASM instance, but performing this task manually is easy and will provide insights into the ASM architecture. The following table walks through the steps of manually creating the ASM instance:

1. As root, open /etc/oratab with a text editor and add an instance with the name +ASM. Exit the root login when done. This step should be completed from each node.

Note: If you create an ASM instance with dbca, you will find that the ASM instance is added to the /etc/oratab file as "+ASM1" or "+ASM2" depending on the node. That configuration is inconsistent with all other cluster databases created by dbca and will not allow use of the racenv script.

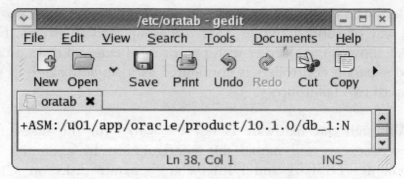

/etc/oratab - gedit

File　Edit　View　Search　Tools　Documents　Help

New　Open　Save　Print　Undo　Redo　Cut　Copy

oratab ✖

```
+ASM:/u01/app/oracle/product/10.1.0/db_1:N
```

Ln 38, Col 1　　　　　INS

2. As oracle, create the supporting directories for the ASM instance. This step should be completed on each node.

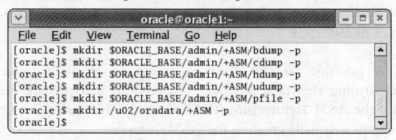

oracle@oracle1:~

File　Edit　View　Terminal　Go　Help

```
[oracle]$ mkdir $ORACLE_BASE/admin/+ASM/bdump -p
[oracle]$ mkdir $ORACLE_BASE/admin/+ASM/cdump -p
[oracle]$ mkdir $ORACLE_BASE/admin/+ASM/hdump -p
[oracle]$ mkdir $ORACLE_BASE/admin/+ASM/udump -p
[oracle]$ mkdir $ORACLE_BASE/admin/+ASM/pfile -p
[oracle]$ mkdir /u02/oradata/+ASM -p
[oracle]$
```

3. From oracle1, as oracle, create the password file in the shared directory as shown.

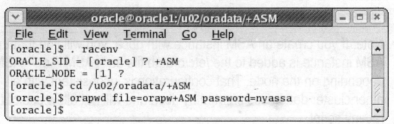

oracle@oracle1:/u02/oradata/+ASM

File　Edit　View　Terminal　Go　Help

```
[oracle]$ . racenv
ORACLE_SID = [oracle] ? +ASM
ORACLE_NODE = [1] ?
[oracle]$ cd /u02/oradata/+ASM
[oracle]$ orapwd file=orapw+ASM password=nyassa
[oracle]$
```

4. Using gedit, create the file $ORACLE_BASE/admin/+ASM/pfile/init+ASM.ora for the ASM database. This step needs to be completed on oracle1 only.

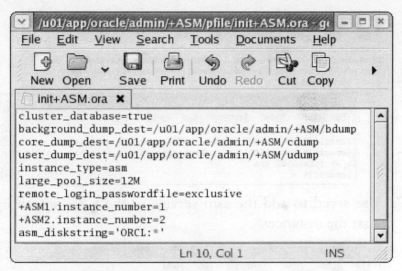

```
cluster_database=true
background_dump_dest=/u01/app/oracle/admin/+ASM/bdump
core_dump_dest=/u01/app/oracle/admin/+ASM/cdump
user_dump_dest=/u01/app/oracle/admin/+ASM/udump
instance_type=asm
large_pool_size=12M
remote_login_passwordfile=exclusive
+ASM1.instance_number=1
+ASM2.instance_number=2
asm_diskstring='ORCL:*'
```

5. From oracle1, create the spfile on the shared disk as shown and exit sqlplus.

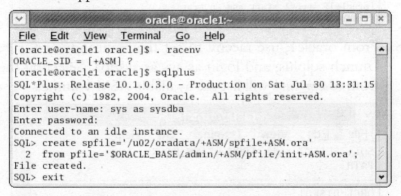

```
[oracle@oracle1 oracle]$ . racenv
ORACLE_SID = [+ASM] ?
[oracle@oracle1 oracle]$ sqlplus

SQL*Plus: Release 10.1.0.3.0 - Production on Sat Jul 30 13:31:15

Copyright (c) 1982, 2004, Oracle.  All rights reserved.

Enter user-name: sys as sysdba
Enter password:
Connected to an idle instance.
SQL> create spfile='/u02/oradata/+ASM/spfile+ASM.ora'
  2  from pfile='$ORACLE_BASE/admin/+ASM/pfile/init+ASM.ora';
File created.
SQL> exit
```

6. From each node, change directory to $ORACLE_HOME/dbs. There, create a symbolic link to the password file and a pointer file to the spfile as shown.

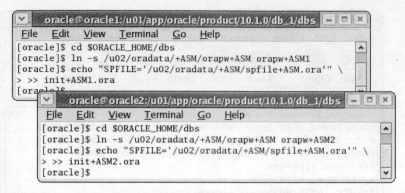

7. Use srvctl to add the asm service to the CRS repository and start the instances.

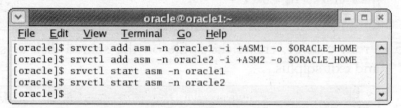

8. From oracle1, use racenv to set the environment for +ASM. Launch sqlplus, and login as sys as sysdba. Selecting the path from *v$asm_disk* will list the available ASM volumes.

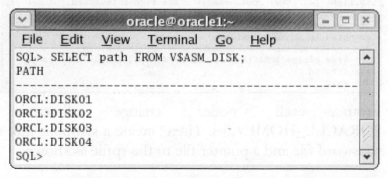

9. Create the diskgroup as shown. Once created, select from *v$asm_diskgroup* for information about the diskgroup just created. Creating the diskgroup from oracle1 automatically adds the following parameter to the spfile:

```
+ASM1.asm_diskgroups='DSKGRP01'
```

This parameter will tell the ASM instance on oracle1 to automatically mount the diskgroup whenever ASM is started. However, it will not mount the diskgroup from the instance on oracle2.

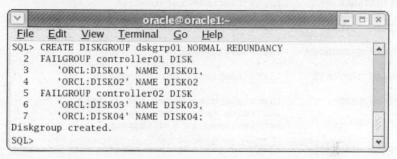

10. From oracle2, use sqlplus to login to the ASM instance as sys. You will find that this instance has not mounted the diskgroup. Do so with the alter diskgroup mount command as shown. This command automatically adds the following parameter to the spfile:

```
+ASM2.asm_diskgroups='DSKGRP01'
```

Now, the diskgroup DSKGRP01 will be mounted by both instances when the ASM instances are started.

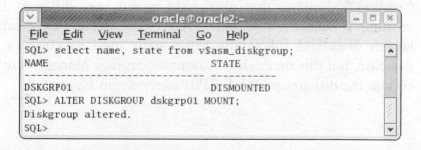

An ASM instance has no datafiles and no data dictionary. Thus, it is never open in the way regular databases are opened. Try selecting from *dba_tables*! The only users that can login to an ASM instance are those with sysdba or sysoper privileges. The

---

following table lists important dynamic performance views available from within the ASM instance:

```
V$PARAMETER          Lists parameters

V$INSTANCE           Lists instance information

V$ASM_CLIENT         Lists each database using ASM diskgroups

V$ASM_DISKGROUP      Lists diskgroups

V$ASM_TEMPLATE       Lists templates per diskgroup

V$ASM_DISK           Lists all discovered ASM volumes,
                     including those that are
                     not included in a diskgroup

V$ASM_OPERATION      Lists active ASM operations

V$ASM_FILE           Lists files present in each mounted ASM diskgroup

V$ASM_ALIAS          Lists aliases (file names) present in
                     each mounted diskgroup
```

```
Note: There is a parallel GV$ view for each of the above listed
views.
       GV$ views provide information for all open instances in the
       cluster.
```

Create a 10g RAC Database That Uses ASM

Creating a database that uses ASM is not very different from creating a database that uses OCFS. To create this database, launch dbca and follow the same steps used to create a 10g database, but this time select Automatic Storage Management and choose the diskgroup DSKGRP01 as shown in Figure 9.8.

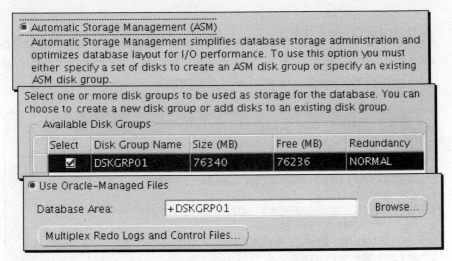

Figure 9.8: *Creating a database that uses ASM from dbca.*

With a database created and using ASM, it is a simple matter to add tablespaces with datafiles stored on ASM. Although it is possible to use explicit names for datafiles, it is far preferable to allow ASM to name the files for you.

To request that ASM name the file, only name the diskgroup in the create tablespace command, for example '+DSKGRP01'. If an entire path and file name is given, such as '+DSKGRP01/last/datafile/my_file01.dbf', the file will be created if the directory exists, but Oracle Managed Files will not be used. This is not desirable because if the tablespace is dropped, the only way to delete the datafile is through one of the ASM instances using the following command:

```
alter diskgroup dskgrp_name drop file
'+<group>.<file#>.<incarnation>'
```

ASM filenames that are created using a standard syntax will be named as follows:

```
+<group>/<database_name>/<file_type>/<tag>.<file#>.<incarnation#>
```

Figure 9.9 demonstrates creating a new tablespace on ASM. The datafile's incarnation# is 5 because the development tablespace had been previously created and dropped.

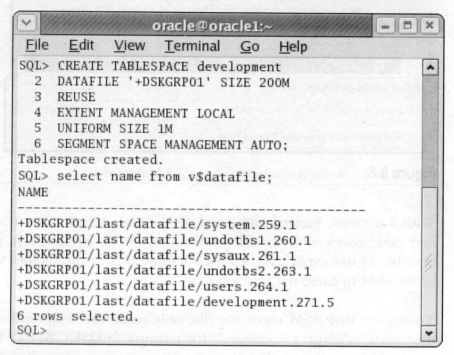

Figure 9.9: *Creating a tablespace on ASM.*

Other file types stored on ASM can be viewed through the commands shown in Figure 9.10.

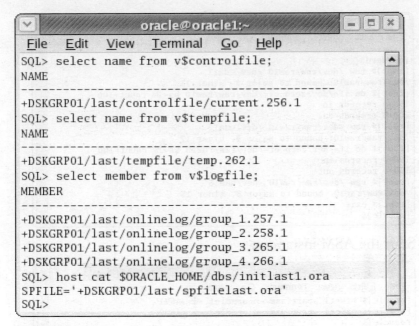

```
                    oracle@oracle1:~                  _ □ ✕
 File   Edit   View   Terminal   Go   Help
SQL> select name from v$controlfile;
NAME
-------------------------------------------------
+DSKGRP01/last/controlfile/current.256.1
SQL> select name from v$tempfile;
NAME
-------------------------------------------------
+DSKGRP01/last/tempfile/temp.262.1
SQL> select member from v$logfile;
MEMBER
-------------------------------------------------
+DSKGRP01/last/onlinelog/group_1.257.1
+DSKGRP01/last/onlinelog/group_2.258.1
+DSKGRP01/last/onlinelog/group_3.265.1
+DSKGRP01/last/onlinelog/group_4.266.1
SQL> host cat $ORACLE_HOME/dbs/initlast1.ora
SPFILE='+DSKGRP01/last/spfilelast.ora'
SQL>
```

Figure 9.10: *Listing other files stored on ASM.*

Simulating the Failure of a Failgroup

An important feature of ASM is although a disk can get wiped out, the database will continue to function -- it is a simple matter to replace a disk.

The following exercise will simulate the total failure of two disks on failgroup01 and the failed disks replaced with new volumes. You may want to create some tables with sample data on your database to demonstrate that nothing is lost. Figure 7.6 in Chapter 7 shows an easy method for creating tables with thousands of rows.

1. Switch to the root user. Bind raw10 to /dev/sda11 (DISK01) and wipe the first 100 megabytes clean. Then, do the same with /dev/sda12 (DISK02). Finally, bind raw10 to an unused partition and exit.

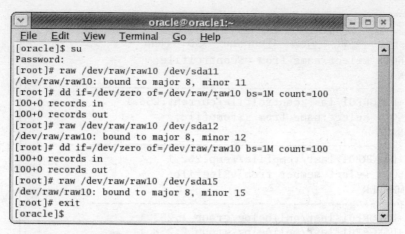

```
[oracle]$ su
Password:
[root]# raw /dev/raw/raw10 /dev/sda11
/dev/raw/raw10: bound to major 8, minor 11
[root]# dd if=/dev/zero of=/dev/raw/raw10 bs=1M count=100
100+0 records in
100+0 records out
[root]# raw /dev/raw/raw10 /dev/sda12
/dev/raw/raw10: bound to major 8, minor 12
[root]# dd if=/dev/zero of=/dev/raw/raw10 bs=1M count=100
100+0 records in
100+0 records out
[root]# raw /dev/raw/raw10 /dev/sda15
/dev/raw/raw10: bound to major 8, minor 15
[root]# exit
[oracle]$
```

2. Start the ASM instances.

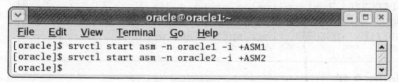

```
[oracle]$ srvctl start asm -n oracle1 -i +ASM1
[oracle]$ srvctl start asm -n oracle2 -i +ASM2
[oracle]$
```

3. Use racenv to set the environment to +ASM. Launch sqlplus and logn sys as sysdba. Verify the condition of the disks as shown. Exit sqlplus.

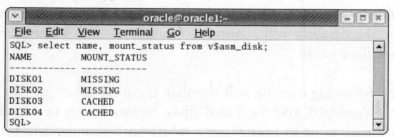

```
SQL> select name, mount_status from v$asm_disk;
NAME          MOUNT_STATUS
------------  ------------
DISK01        MISSING
DISK02        MISSING
DISK03        CACHED
DISK04        CACHED
SQL>
```

4. You can start the database at any time now with either srvctl or sqlplus. It may be preferable to use sqlplus for this first startup after an intentional crash. (When I use srvctl at this point my system tends to hang). Once the database is open, verify any objects made previously. All the data is there; if it were not, the database would not open on either node!

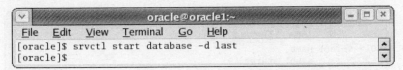

```
oracle@oracle1:~
File  Edit  View  Terminal  Go  Help
[oracle]$ srvctl start database -d last
[oracle]$
```

5. The next steps will add disk volumes to restore those that were lost. There is no reason to shutdown either ASM or the database using ASM storage. Start on oracle1 by switching to the root user. Follow the steps taken in the image above, first on oracle1, then on oracle2. Exit the root login from each when finished.

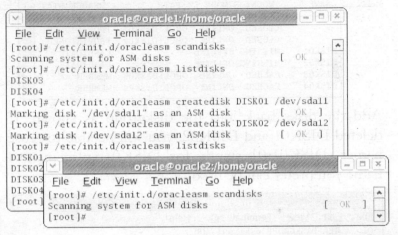

```
oracle@oracle1:/home/oracle
File  Edit  View  Terminal  Go  Help
[root]# /etc/init.d/oracleasm scandisks
Scanning system for ASM disks              [  OK  ]
[root]# /etc/init.d/oracleasm listdisks
DISK03
DISK04
[root]# /etc/init.d/oracleasm createdisk DISK01 /dev/sda11
Marking disk "/dev/sda11" as an ASM disk   [  OK  ]
[root]# /etc/init.d/oracleasm createdisk DISK02 /dev/sda12
Marking disk "/dev/sda12" as an ASM disk   [  OK  ]
[root]# /etc/init.d/oracleasm listdisks
DISK01
DISK02      oracle@oracle2:/home/oracle
DISK03  File  Edit  View  Terminal  Go  Help
DISK04  [root]# /etc/init.d/oracleasm scandisks
[root]  Scanning system for ASM disks       [  OK  ]
        [root]#
```

6. As oracle, use racenv to set the environment for +ASM. Login sys as sysdba. Run the select statement shown. There are two possible outcomes. ASM is supposed to delete the disks named DISK01 and DISK02. Perhaps it has not yet completed that task.

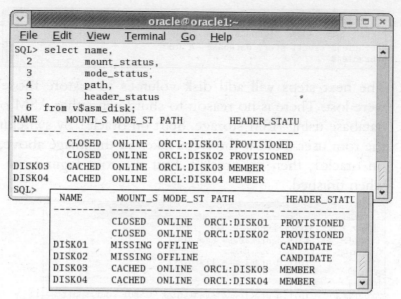

7. Add the disks back into the diskgroup as shown. If ASM deleted DISK01 and DISK02, you will be able to reuse those names. DISK01r01 stands for DISK01replacement01. Any name you prefer can be used.

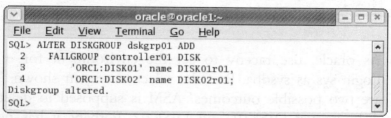

8. Quickly query *v$asm_operations* and you will find that it is working to rebalance the extents across the newly added disks of FAILGROUP01.

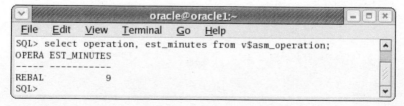

Conclusion

SCREEEEECH...OUCH!!! What was that!? Oh...it was the end of the chapter. Where's the Conclusion...Transition?

Instances on 10g CRS and Upgrading a 9i Database

Managing a 9i RAC Database on 10g Clusterware

The key to managing a 9i database after the 10g CRS has been installed is to use the 9i version of srvctl, sqlplus, rman, etc. to start, stop and maintain the 9i instances.

Use the racenv script to ensure the correct version of a given application is used to manage a given database, and use the Linux which command to double check that the correct version is accessed for a given database. Switching from a 9i database to a 10g database is just a matter of using racenv to change the environmental variables. It is really that simple!

The 10g version of gsd will provide service to the 9i srvctl just fine. The 9i version of the gsdctl script was intentionally disabled in Chapter 8 because it should not be used to manage the 10g gsd service.

Registering the 9i Service with a 10g Listener

It is extremely easy to register a 9i database with a 10g listener. Simply start it up with the 9i version of srvctl, and use the 10g version of lsnrctl status LISTENER_<node_name> to check the service.

When starting the 9i database, the error message "PRKP-1040 Failed to get the status of the listeners associated with instance…" should be ignored! The database will start normally and will be served by the 10g listener even though this message may appear.

The tnsnames.ora file in the 9i oracle home will serve the 9i clients that need to connect to 9i instances. Edit the 9i tnsnames.ora file so that the host names read "vip-oracle1" and "vip-oracle2". There is no need to edit the tnsnames.ora file in the 10g oracle home.

Fixing a Shared Object File

If a 9i database will be run on a 10g cluster for an extended period of time, Oracle suggests, in its release notes for 10g (Part number B10817-04), replacing the 10g version of libcmdll.so with the 9i version.

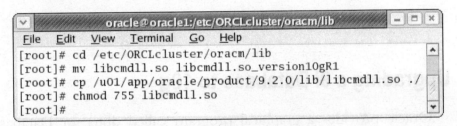

Figure 10.1: *Replacing the 10g version of libcmdll.so.*

Figure 10.1 demonstrates backing up the 10g version of this file and replacing it with the 9i version. This should be done as root on both nodes. After this is completed, use the 10g srvctl to stop nodeapps on each node; then start nodeapps on each node.

Oracle does not explain the reason for this change, nor does it explain what will happen if it is not done. I have run 9i databases on a 10g CRS both with and without this step and no noticeable difference was detected.

If a 9i database is upgraded and no other 9i databases are to be used, restore the original 10g version of this file and restart nodeapps on each node.

Registering a 9i Database using srvctl if necessary

If the CRS has been wiped out and rebuilt by using the instructions in Appendix G, the previously created 9i instances will not be included any longer. Use the 9i or 10g srvctl to find out if the instances are registered:

```
srvctl config database -d test
```

If the database is missing, just add it back in with 9i srvctl:

```
srvctl add database -d test -o $ORACLE_HOME
srvctl add instance -d test -i west1 -n oracle1
srvctl add instance -d test -i west2 -n oracle2
```

Upgrading a 9i Database to 10g

Oracle provides a graphical program called dbua, or Database Upgrade Assistant, that can be used to upgrade a database. If you choose to use dbua, make sure you are not using the 9i version because its purpose is to upgrade older databases to version 9i. The 9i version and 10g versions look nearly identical unless you carefully read the welcome screen.

This book will not show a demonstration of the dbua because it does not teach much about the upgrade process. Also, the 10g dbua will not work unless a modification is made to the script that launches the program. The solution for this problem is documented in Appendix C.

The following table walks through the steps taken to manually upgrade a 9i database named TEST to a 10g database. Before running through these steps, it is a good idea to shutdown any other instances that may be running, including any +ASM instances.

1. For an upgrade there are times in which you will want to be certain you are accessing a particular oracle home. Therefore, it is a good idea to have two variables that are hard coded to these directories. Add these variables to the end of the oracle user's *.bash_profile* as shown. Log out of the operating system and log back in as oracle user.

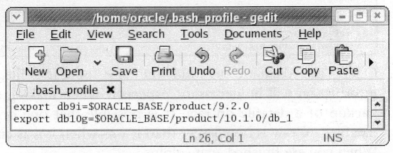

2. Use racenv to set the environment, then startup the database that is about to be upgraded.

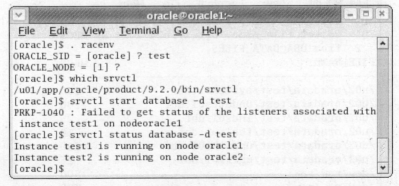

3. Using sqlplus, login to the database as the sys user. Spool the results of the upgrade diagnostic script into a file. Even though the current $ORACLE_HOME is for the 9i directory, you are accessing a script in the 10g home.

The script will take a minute or so to produce the results. When it is finished, issue the command spool off to stop the spooling. At this point, open the spooled file in a text editor and read its recommendations for upgrading the database. Use these recommendations as a basis for editing the pfile to support the upgrade.

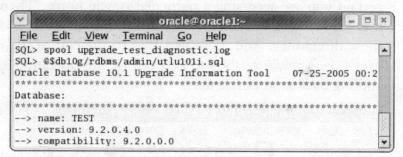

4. Query the database to find the size of each file. This information will be necessary, especially when making a cold backup of a datafile on raw. It is possible that one or more datafiles on raw is now larger than it was when it was created. When you are finished, exit sqlplus.

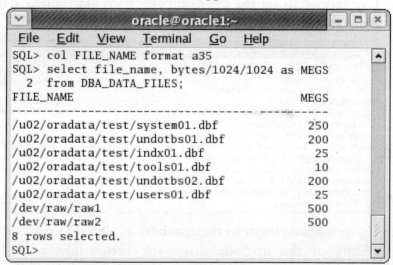

5. Use *srvctl* to shutdown the database on both nodes, and remove the database configuration from the CRS repository.

This will make the test database unavailable to the 9i *srvctl* command.

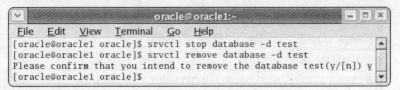

```
oracle@oracle1:~
File  Edit  View  Terminal  Go  Help
[oracle@oracle1 oracle]$ srvctl stop database -d test
[oracle@oracle1 oracle]$ srvctl remove database -d test
Please confirm that you intend to remove the database test(y/[n]) y
[oracle@oracle1 oracle]$
```

6. Choose the method you prefer for backing up the database. My preference for a database in noarchivelog mode is a cold backup, as shown. For the partitions on raw, the *dd* copy method should be used. Copy more bytes of data than the size of the file. In this case, 64000 8k blocks is equal to 500 megabytes. 64 extra blocks are copied to ensure the file is complete. You will find copying with *dd* from raw is much faster than copying with *cp* from a file system.

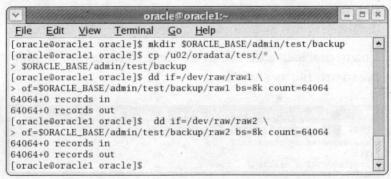

```
oracle@oracle1:~
File  Edit  View  Terminal  Go  Help
[oracle@oracle1 oracle]$ mkdir $ORACLE_BASE/admin/test/backup
[oracle@oracle1 oracle]$ cp /u02/oradata/test/* \
> $ORACLE_BASE/admin/test/backup
[oracle@oracle1 oracle]$ dd if=/dev/raw/raw1 \
> of=$ORACLE_BASE/admin/test/backup/raw1 bs=8k count=64064
64064+0 records in
64064+0 records out
[oracle@oracle1 oracle]$ dd if=/dev/raw/raw2 \
> of=$ORACLE_BASE/admin/test/backup/raw2 bs=8k count=64064
64064+0 records in
64064+0 records out
[oracle@oracle1 oracle]$
```

7. Use the su command to switch to the root user. Open the file /etc/oratab in gedit and change the oracle home for the database being upgraded to the 10g oracle home. Complete this step on each node.

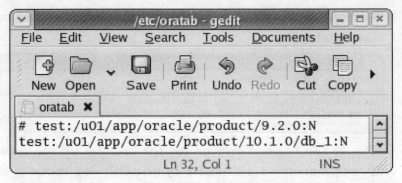

```
# test:/u01/app/oracle/product/9.2.0:N
test:/u01/app/oracle/product/10.1.0/db_1:N
```

8. On oracle1, exit the root login. Run the racenv script to set the environment, which will change the $ORACLE_HOME and $PATH to the new home. Change directories to the directory for the test database files. Verify that the orapwd about to be used is the 10g version. Create a password file as shown. Change to the dbs directory and create two links to the password file. The second link will be used when the database is run as a single instance during the upgrade.

   From oracle2, exit the root login and create a link to the password file as shown.

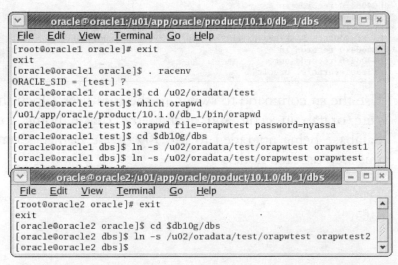

```
[root@oracle1 oracle]# exit
exit
[oracle@oracle1 oracle]$ . racenv
ORACLE_SID = [test] ?
[oracle@oracle1 oracle]$ cd /u02/oradata/test
[oracle@oracle1 test]$ which orapwd
/u01/app/oracle/product/10.1.0/db_1/bin/orapwd
[oracle@oracle1 test]$ orapwd file=orapwtest password=nyassa
[oracle@oracle1 test]$ cd $db10g/dbs
[oracle@oracle1 dbs]$ ln -s /u02/oradata/test/orapwtest orapwtest1
[oracle@oracle1 dbs]$ ln -s /u02/oradata/test/orapwtest orapwtest
```

```
[root@oracle2 oracle]# exit
exit
[oracle@oracle2 oracle]$ cd $db10g/dbs
[oracle@oracle2 dbs]$ ln -s /u02/oradata/test/orapwtest orapwtest2
[oracle@oracle2 dbs]$
```

9. Each node has a text file that points to the spfile. This file should be moved from the 9i home to the 10g home.

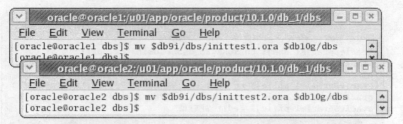

```
oracle@oracle1:/u01/app/oracle/product/10.1.0/db_1/dbs
File  Edit  View  Terminal  Go  Help
[oracle@oracle1 dbs]$ mv $db9i/dbs/inittest1.ora $db10g/dbs
[oracle@oracle1 dbs]$
```

```
oracle@oracle2:/u01/app/oracle/product/10.1.0/db_1/dbs
File  Edit  View  Terminal  Go  Help
[oracle@oracle2 dbs]$ mv $db9i/dbs/inittest2.ora $db10g/dbs
[oracle@oracle2 dbs]$
```

10. When a database is created with dbca, a text parameter file is created with a path and name like $ORACLE_BASE/admin/<sid>/pfile/init.ora.nnnnnnnnnn. This file will work perfectly for the database to be upgraded.

Copy the file to a new file as shown and export an environmental variable $PFILE to match the path and filename of the new file. Then, edit the file with gedit And consult the *upgrade_test_diagnostic.log* previously created to make the necessary changes to the parameters. The database will be opened as a non-cluster database during the upgrade process.

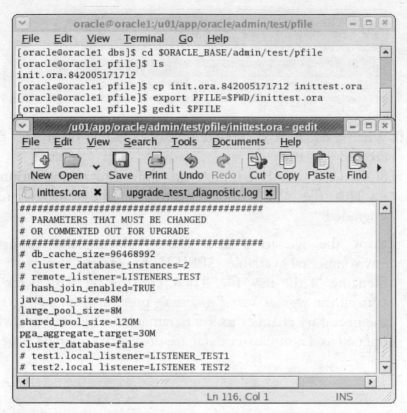

11. Change directories to the oracle user's home directory. Use oraenv to set the environment. Startup the database with the UPGRADE keyword.

🔔 Note: you should be using the 10g version of SQLPLUS.

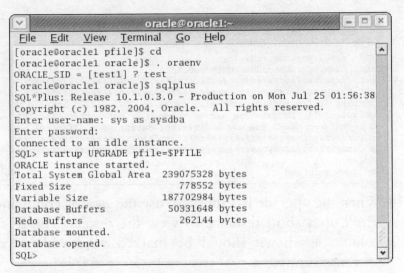

```
[oracle@oracle1 pfile]$ cd
[oracle@oracle1 oracle]$ . oraenv
ORACLE_SID = [test1] ? test
[oracle@oracle1 oracle]$ sqlplus
SQL*Plus: Release 10.1.0.3.0 - Production on Mon Jul 25 01:56:38
Copyright (c) 1982, 2004, Oracle.  All rights reserved.
Enter user-name: sys as sysdba
Enter password:
Connected to an idle instance.
SQL> startup UPGRADE pfile=$PFILE
ORACLE instance started.
Total System Global Area  239075328 bytes
Fixed Size                   778552 bytes
Variable Size             187702984 bytes
Database Buffers           50331648 bytes
Redo Buffers                 262144 bytes
Database mounted.
Database opened.
SQL>
```

12. Create the sysaux tablespace as shown. This tablespace is required for a 10g database. It can be sized from 70 megabytes to 5 gigabytes. For a small test database, 300 megabytes is more than enough.

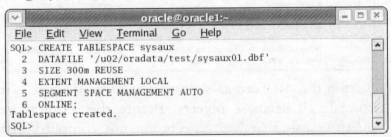

```
SQL> CREATE TABLESPACE sysaux
  2  DATAFILE '/u02/oradata/test/sysaux01.dbf'
  3  SIZE 300m REUSE
  4  EXTENT MANAGEMENT LOCAL
  5  SEGMENT SPACE MANAGEMENT AUTO
  6  ONLINE;
Tablespace created.
SQL>
```

13. There are four upgrade scripts available with names that match the version of the database to be upgraded: u0800060.sql, u0801070.sql, u0900010.sql, u0902000.sql.

Spool a log of the database upgrade and run the u0902000.sql as shown. It will stream by quickly for about an hour. When it reaches the end, it will appear to hang, but it is still working (use the system monitor to check CPU activity).

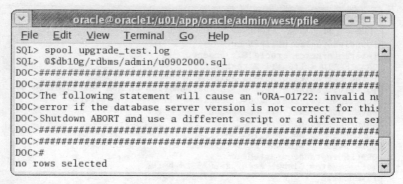

```
oracle@oracle1:/u01/app/oracle/admin/west/pfile
 File   Edit   View   Terminal   Go   Help
SQL> spool upgrade_test.log
SQL> @$db10g/rdbms/admin/u0902000.sql
DOC>#############################################################
DOC>#############################################################
DOC>The following statement will cause an "ORA-01722: invalid nu
DOC>error if the database server version is not correct for this
DOC>Shutdown ABORT and use a different script or a different ser
DOC>#############################################################
DOC>#############################################################
DOC>#
no rows selected
```

14. When the upgrade has finished, use the *spool off* command and scroll up a short distance to view the results. The STATUS column as shown should be marked valid with a version 10.1.x as shown.

Now, shutdown the database.

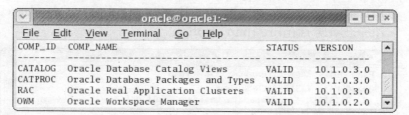

```
oracle@oracle1:~
 File   Edit   View   Terminal   Go   Help
COMP_ID   COMP_NAME                          STATUS    VERSION
-------   --------------------------------   --------  ----------
CATALOG   Oracle Database Catalog Views      VALID     10.1.0.3.0
CATPROC   Oracle Database Packages and Types VALID     10.1.0.3.0
RAC       Oracle Real Application Clusters   VALID     10.1.0.3.0
OWM       Oracle Workspace Manager           VALID     10.1.0.2.0
```

15. Startup the database as shown. The *utlrp.sql* script is used to compile all database objects. Before the script is run, the query reveals that 308 objects are not compiled. After the *utlrp.sql* script completes, rerun the query to determine the count of invalid objects.

Shutdown the database and exit sqlplus

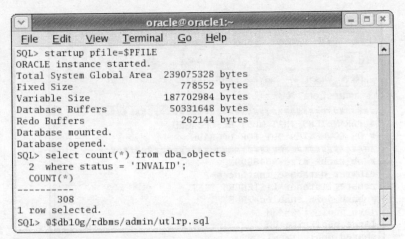

```
SQL> startup pfile=$PFILE
ORACLE instance started.
Total System Global Area   239075328 bytes
Fixed Size                    778552 bytes
Variable Size              187702984 bytes
Database Buffers            50331648 bytes
Redo Buffers                  262144 bytes
Database mounted.
Database opened.
SQL> select count(*) from dba_objects
  2  where status = 'INVALID';
  COUNT(*)
----------
       308
1 row selected.
SQL> @$db10g/rdbms/admin/utlrp.sql
```

16. Run the *update_tns.sh* script to add the database to the 10g tnsnames.ora file. This step must be competed on each node.

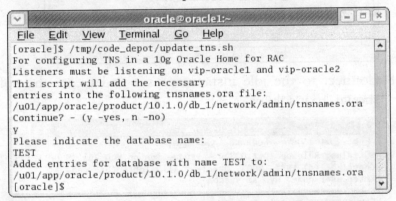

```
[oracle]$ /tmp/code_depot/update_tns.sh
For configuring TNS in a 10g Oracle Home for RAC
Listeners must be listening on vip-oracle1 and vip-oracle2
This script will add the necessary
entries into the following tnsnames.ora file:
/u01/app/oracle/product/10.1.0/db_1/network/admin/tnsnames.ora
Continue? - (y -yes, n -no)
y
Please indicate the database name:
TEST
Added entries for database with name TEST to:
/u01/app/oracle/product/10.1.0/db_1/network/admin/tnsnames.ora
[oracle]$
```

17. Open the parameter file with the command gedit $PFILE and make the changes as shown. The compatible parameter should be changed to reflect the upgrade. Once the database is started with the compatible parameter for this version, it cannot be rolled back to the previous version.

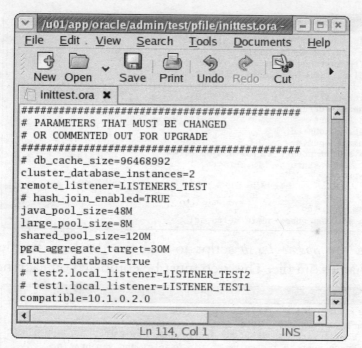

```
##############################################
# PARAMETERS THAT MUST BE CHANGED
# OR COMMENTED OUT FOR UPGRADE
##############################################
# db_cache_size=96468992
cluster_database_instances=2
remote_listener=LISTENERS_TEST
# hash_join_enabled=TRUE
java_pool_size=48M
large_pool_size=8M
shared_pool_size=120M
pga_aggregate_target=30M
cluster_database=true
# test2.local_listener=LISTENER_TEST2
# test1.local_listener=LISTENER_TEST1
compatible=10.1.0.2.0
```

18. Connect to the idle instance as sys and create the spfile as shown. Exit sqlplus.

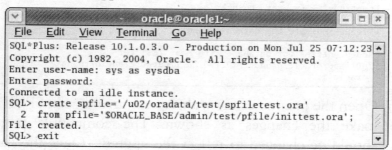

```
SQL*Plus: Release 10.1.0.3.0 - Production on Mon Jul 25 07:12:23
Copyright (c) 1982, 2004, Oracle.  All rights reserved.
Enter user-name: sys as sysdba
Enter password:
Connected to an idle instance.
SQL> create spfile='/u02/oradata/test/spfiletest.ora'
  2  from pfile='$ORACLE_BASE/admin/test/pfile/inittest.ora';
File created.
SQL> exit
```

19. Use srvctl to add the database back in as a 10g database.

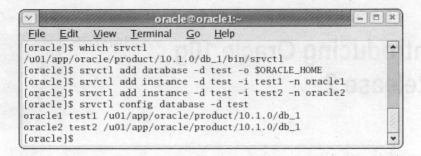

```
[oracle]$ which srvctl
/u01/app/oracle/product/10.1.0/db_1/bin/srvctl
[oracle]$ srvctl add database -d test -o $ORACLE_HOME
[oracle]$ srvctl add instance -d test -i test1 -n oracle1
[oracle]$ srvctl add instance -d test -i test2 -n oracle2
[oracle]$ srvctl config database -d test
oracle1 test1 /u01/app/oracle/product/10.1.0/db_1
oracle2 test2 /u01/app/oracle/product/10.1.0/db_1
[oracle]$
```

At this point, it is a very good idea to use sqlplus to startup and shutdown each instance, one node at a time. No pfile should be indicated in the startup command. This will ensure all steps were completed and each node is ready.

Conclusion

As you have seen, upgrading a 9i RAC database to a 10g RAC database is an excellent exercise for learning oracle file architecture. In the next chapter, Oracle 10g Release 2 is introduced.

Introducing Oracle 10g Release 2

Oracle 10g Release 2 for Linux has been made available for download just in time for it to be included, at least briefly, in this book. Linux was the first operating system for which Oracle 10g Release 2 was available for download. This speaks volumes for Oracle Corporation's recognition of the stability and value that Linux offers as a platform for the Oracle database.

Upgrading Cluster Ready Services to Release 2

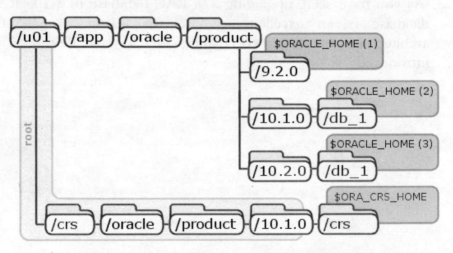

Figure 11.1: *OFA for 9i, 10g release 1 and 10g release 2.*

Figure 11.1 demonstrates the OFA directory structure with three releases installed. Note that the CRS still has a directory of "10.1.0" in its path. This is because only one $ORA_CRS_HOME can exist on a node. Thus, to install the software in an upgrade scenario like this one, it has to be installed into the current $ORA_CRS_HOME directory. There is a way to get around this and that is to use dbca to uninstall the software in $ORA_CRS_HOME, then to install the release 2 version into a more properly named directory. The following pages will demonstrate an upgrade install with no concern regarding the directory name.

The following table steps through the install of Oracle 10g Release 2 CRS:

1. Ensure all databases and the ASM are shutdown and disabled or they will automatically restart when the 10g Clusterware install is finished.

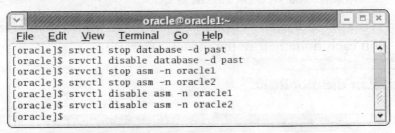

```
oracle@oracle1:~
File  Edit  View  Terminal  Go  Help
[oracle]$ srvctl stop database -d past
[oracle]$ srvctl disable database -d past
[oracle]$ srvctl stop asm -n oracle1
[oracle]$ srvctl stop asm -n oracle2
[oracle]$ srvctl disable asm -n oracle1
[oracle]$ srvctl disable asm -n oracle2
[oracle]$
```

2. Use srvctl to stop the nodeapps on both nodes. If this command hangs, type ctl+c and run it a second time. Use the command srvctl status nodeapps -n <nodename> to ensure the listeners are not running.

   Next, launch the netca program and delete the listeners.

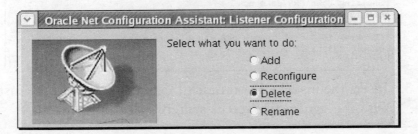

Oracle Net Configuration Assistant: Listener Configuration

Select what you want to do:
- ○ Add
- ○ Reconfigure
- ● Delete
- ○ Rename

3. Backup these useful scripts because they will be overwritten by the release 2 install. Complete this step as oracle on each node.

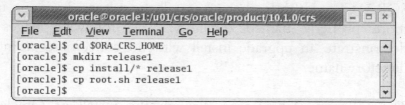

```
oracle@oracle1:/u01/crs/oracle/product/10.1.0/crs
File  Edit  View  Terminal  Go  Help
[oracle]$ cd $ORA_CRS_HOME
[oracle]$ mkdir release1
[oracle]$ cp install/* release1
[oracle]$ cp root.sh release1
[oracle]$
```

4. Insert the CD for 10g Release 2 Clusterware. There is a preupdate script that must be run as root. I have found that this script hangs. To prevent it from hanging, run the /etc/init.d/init.cssd stop script as shown. Eject the CD and complete this step on the next node.

   The preupdate.sh script must complete without intervention on each node before the install.

   Exit the root login.

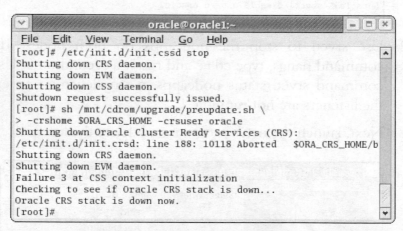

```
oracle@oracle1:~
File  Edit  View  Terminal  Go  Help
[root]# /etc/init.d/init.cssd stop
Shutting down CRS daemon.
Shutting down EVM daemon.
Shutting down CSS daemon.
Shutdown request successfully issued.
[root]# sh /mnt/cdrom/upgrade/preupdate.sh \
> -crshome $ORA_CRS_HOME -crsuser oracle
Shutting down Oracle Cluster Ready Services (CRS):
/etc/init.d/init.crsd: line 188: 10118 Aborted    $ORA_CRS_HOME/b
Shutting down CRS daemon.
Shutting down EVM daemon.
Failure 3 at CSS context initialization
Checking to see if Oracle CRS stack is down...
Oracle CRS stack is down now.
[root]#
```

5. Insert the install CD on oracle1 again, and launch the installer with the -ignoreSysPrereqs switch.

6. The software will find the current directory for $ORA_CRS_HOME and will use it. You cannot modify the directory in an upgrade install like this one.

> 🔔 Note: for a non-upgrade install, Oracle suggests using the following directory path:
>
> /u01/crs/oracle/product/10/crs

7. If you create this directory structure, remember to make root own the directories leading up to the final crs directory, with only root having write permission on those directories.

8. Ensure oracle2 is checked and click next.

9. The prerequisite page is self-explanatory. The first three checks will likely fail; just add a check to each checkbox. The

final checkbox "Checking Cluster Synchronization Services" must succeed on its own. If it does not, quit the install and rerun the preupdate.sh script on each node.

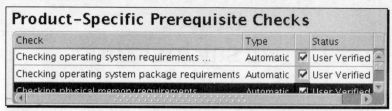

10. With the release 2 installer, configuration script(s) appear in a table as seen above. Run the rootupgrade script as shown, first on oracle1, then on oracle2. Be patient. These scripts can take a few minutes to finish.

After the scripts have run and you have clicked through to the next step, the installer will check that everything worked, then exit.

Run *crs_status* command to verify the services gsd, ons, and vip are online on each node. No other service should be online.

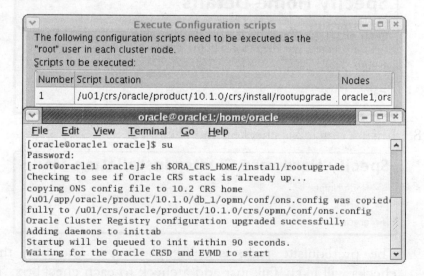

Installing 10g Release 2 Database Software

The oracle user account will need an updated version of its default variables. Figure 11.2 shows the variables after being updated for Oracle 10g Release 2. The file should be updated on each node.

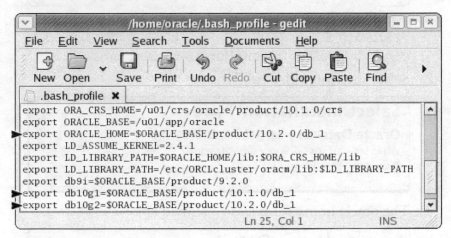

Figure 11.2: *Change the default variables in ~oracle/.bash_profile.*

The following table will walk through the steps of installing Oracle Database Software Release 2.

1. Insert the CD for Oracle Database Software Release 2 and launch the installer.

2. Select the Enterprise Edition.

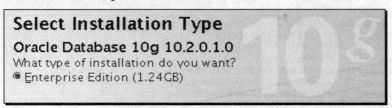

3. The oracle home for release 2 should appear as shown.

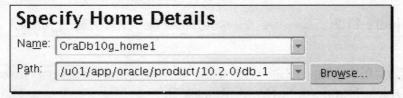

4. Ensure oracle2 is checked and click next.

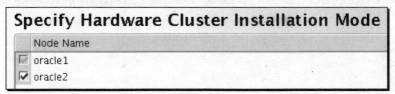

5. On this prerequisite-check screen, you can either check the boxes where it fails, or click "next" and get a warning.

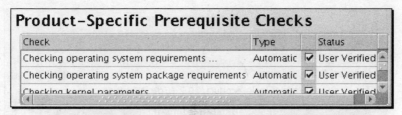

Product-Specific Prerequisite Checks

Check	Type	Status
Checking operating system requirements ...	Automatic	☑ User Verified
Checking operating system package requirements	Automatic	☑ User Verified
Checking kernel parameters	Automatic	☑ User Verified

6. Choose No to upgrade an existing database.

Upgrade an Existing Database

Do you want to perform an upgrade now?
  ⦿ No
  ○ Yes

7. Choose to install database software only. The possibility of configuring ASM at this point is new.

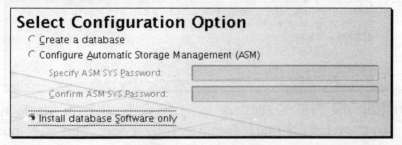

Select Configuration Option
  ○ Create a database
  ○ Configure Automatic Storage Management (ASM)

    Specify ASM SYS Password: [   ]

    Confirm ASM SYS Password: [   ]

  ⦿ Install database Software only

8. As in previous installs, the final step is to run the *root.sh* script. Be sure to run the script in the release 2 oracle home directory. Replace previous versions of dbhome, oraenv, and coraenv by answering 'y' to the prompts. This step must be completed on each node.

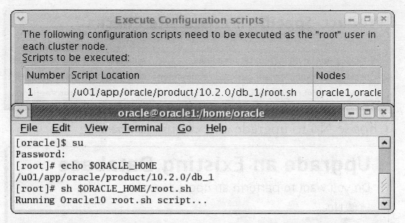

9. The installation should finish without any trouble

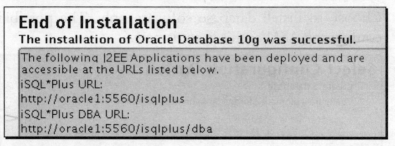

10. Edit the /etc/oratab file to change the default oracle_home to the release 2 oracle home as shown here. This step must be done as root on each node.

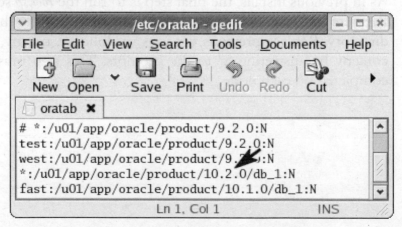

11. Launch the release 2 netca program and install the listeners.

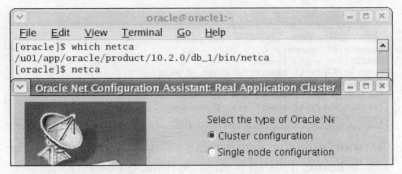

12. It is a good idea to backup the CRS and voting files right after the install.

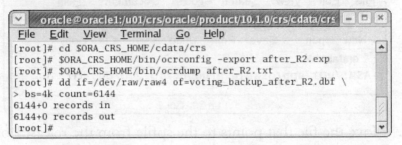

Moving ASM to Release 2

With release 2 completely installed, the first step to take is to move ASM to the release 2 home directory. To start this process, ensure ASM and any dependent databases are still shut down.

The following table steps though moving ASM to the release 2 oracle home:

1. Remove the ASM service for each node from the CRS using the 10g release 1 srvctl.

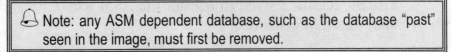

Note: any ASM dependent database, such as the database "past" seen in the image, must first be removed.

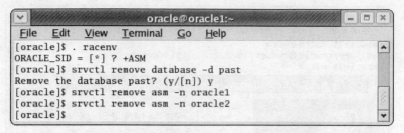

```
[oracle]$ . racenv
ORACLE_SID = [*] ? +ASM
[oracle]$ srvctl remove database -d past
Remove the database past? (y/[n]) y
[oracle]$ srvctl remove asm -n oracle1
[oracle]$ srvctl remove asm -n oracle2
[oracle]$
```

2. As root, edit the /etc/oratab to update +ASM for the new oracle home. This step must be done on each node.

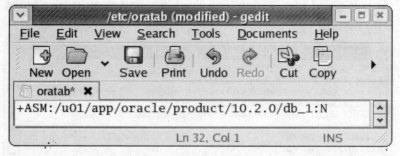

```
+ASM:/u01/app/oracle/product/10.2.0/db_1:N
```

3. Move the file that points to the spfile from the release1 oracle home to the release 2 oracle home. Recreate the link to the password file. This step must be completed on each node using the appropriate file names as shown.

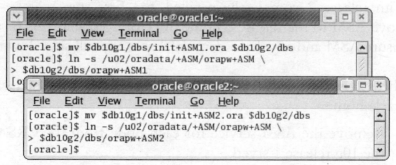

```
[oracle]$ mv $db10g1/dbs/init+ASM1.ora $db10g2/dbs
[oracle]$ ln -s /u02/oradata/+ASM/orapw+ASM \
> $db10g2/dbs/orapw+ASM1
[oracle]$ mv $db10g1/dbs/init+ASM2.ora $db10g2/dbs
[oracle]$ ln -s /u02/oradata/+ASM/orapw+ASM \
> $db10g2/dbs/orapw+ASM2
[oracle]$
```

4. Use the release 2 srvctl to register the ASM with CRS and to start the ASM instances.

```
oracle@oracle1:~
 File   Edit   View   Terminal   Go   Help
[oracle]$ . racenv
ORACLE_SID = [oracle] ? +ASM
ORACLE_NODE = [1] ?
[oracle]$ which srvctl
/u01/app/oracle/product/10.2.0/db_1/bin/srvctl
[oracle]$ srvctl add asm -n oracle1 -i +ASM1 -o $ORACLE_HOME
[oracle]$ srvctl add asm -n oracle2 -i +ASM2 -o $ORACLE_HOME
[oracle]$ srvctl start asm -n oracle1
[oracle]$ srvctl start asm -n oracle2
[oracle]$
```

Upgrading a 10g Release 1 Database to 10g Release 2

The steps for upgrading a database to 10g release 2 are similar to those demonstrated in the 9i to 10g upgrade in Chapter 10. The following table will walk through the steps of the upgrade process for a 10g release 1 database named PAST that is stored on ASM.

You may prefer to use sqlplus to start up your database on only one node to avoid problems that could come from adding a database to and then removing a database from the CRS with srvctl.

1. With the PAST database started up, spool the upgrade diagnostic script as shown.

   Shutdown the database, and if necessary, remove the database from CRS with srvctl.

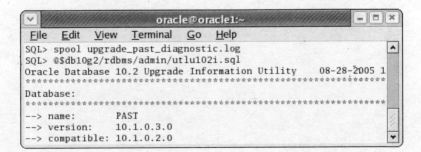

```
oracle@oracle1:~
 File   Edit   View   Terminal   Go   Help
SQL> spool upgrade_past_diagnostic.log
SQL> @$db10g2/rdbms/admin/utlu102i.sql
Oracle Database 10.2 Upgrade Information Utility    08-28-2005 1
************************************************************************
Database:
************************************************************************
--> name:        PAST
--> version:     10.1.0.3.0
--> compatible:  10.1.0.2.0
```

2. Create a backup directory $ORACLE_BASE/admin/<db_name>/backup.

   Use racenv to set the environment for the database. Launch RMAN and startup mount as shown. The backup of a database in mount state using RMAN is equivalent to a cold backup.

   When the backup is finished, issue the shutdown immediate command and exit.

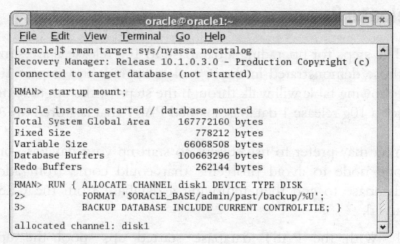

```
oracle@oracle1:~
File   Edit   View   Terminal   Go   Help
[oracle]$ rman target sys/nyassa nocatalog
Recovery Manager: Release 10.1.0.3.0 - Production Copyright (c)
connected to target database (not started)

RMAN> startup mount;

Oracle instance started / database mounted
Total System Global Area     167772160 bytes
Fixed Size                        778212 bytes
Variable Size                   66068508 bytes
Database Buffers               100663296 bytes
Redo Buffers                       262144 bytes

RMAN> RUN { ALLOCATE CHANNEL disk1 DEVICE TYPE DISK
2>            FORMAT '$ORACLE_BASE/admin/past/backup/%U';
3>            BACKUP DATABASE INCLUDE CURRENT CONTROLFILE; }

allocated channel: disk1
```

3. From each node, move the *initpast.ora* pointer files to the new oracle home. Create a new password file using 10g release 2 version of *orapwd*.

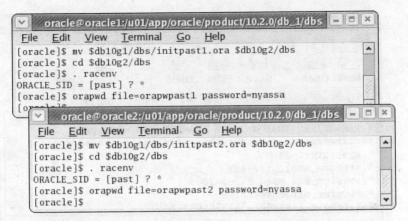

```
oracle@oracle1:/u01/app/oracle/product/10.2.0/db_1/dbs

File   Edit   View   Terminal   Go   Help
[oracle]$ mv $db10g1/dbs/initpast1.ora $db10g2/dbs
[oracle]$ cd $db10g2/dbs
[oracle]$ . racenv
ORACLE_SID = [past] ? *
[oracle]$ orapwd file=orapwpast1 password=nyassa
[o
```

```
oracle@oracle2:/u01/app/oracle/product/10.2.0/db_1/dbs

File   Edit   View   Terminal   Go   Help
[oracle]$ mv $db10g1/dbs/initpast2.ora $db10g2/dbs
[oracle]$ cd $db10g2/dbs
[oracle]$ . racenv
ORACLE_SID = [past] ? *
[oracle]$ orapwd file=orapwpast2 password=nyassa
[oracle]$
```

4. Instead of using a copy of the original pfile, this time a new pfile will be created. To do this, launch sqlplus. Login sys as sysdba and create a pfile as shown. It is not necessary to start the database if the path and filename of the spfile are included as shown.

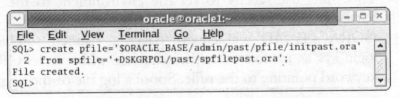

```
oracle@oracle1:~

File   Edit   View   Terminal   Go   Help
SQL> create pfile='$ORACLE_BASE/admin/past/pfile/initpast.ora'
  2  from spfile='+DSKGRP01/past/spfilepast.ora';
File created.
SQL>
```

5. Using the ~/upgrade_<db_name>_diagnostic.log file that was spooled, find the parameters that need to be changed and open the pfile and change them as shown. If a *remote_listener* is defined, it must be commented out as shown.

As root, open the /etc/oratab file with an editor and change the oracle home directory for the PAST database to the release 2 home. This should be done on both nodes.

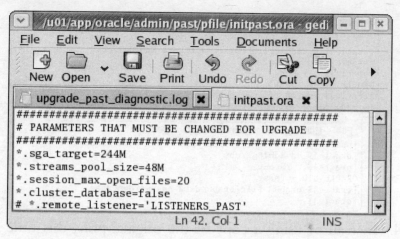

```
################################################
# PARAMETERS THAT MUST BE CHANGED FOR UPGRADE
################################################
*.sga_target=244M
*.streams_pool_size=48M
*.session_max_open_files=20
*.cluster_database=false
# *.remote_listener='LISTENERS_PAST'
```

6. Use the export command to define an environmental variable PFILE that equals the path and filename for the parameter file created in the previous step.

This time, use racenv to set the environment to the PAST database located in the release 2 oracle home ($ORACLE_SID will equal "past1"). Launch sqlplus and login sys as sysdba. Start the database with the UPGRADE keyword pointing to the pfile. Spool a log file of the upgrade.

Oracle 10g Release 2 has just one upgrade script for all versions being upgraded. It does the work of selecting the appropriate sub-scripts to run depending on the version of the database being upgraded.

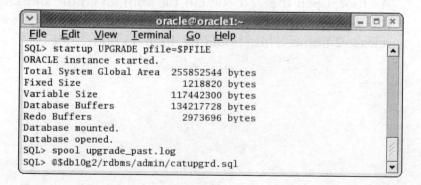

```
SQL> startup UPGRADE pfile=$PFILE
ORACLE instance started.
Total System Global Area    255852544 bytes
Fixed Size                    1218820 bytes
Variable Size               117442300 bytes
Database Buffers            134217728 bytes
Redo Buffers                  2973696 bytes
Database mounted.
Database opened.
SQL> spool upgrade_past.log
SQL> @$db10g2/rdbms/admin/catupgrd.sql
```

7. When the upgrade completes, scroll up and find the results table to ensure the upgrade was successful.

Shutdown the database. Startup the database using the pfile=$PFILE, but without the UPGRADE keyword. After startup, run the script @$db10g2/rdbms/admin/utlrp.sql to compile all of the database objects.

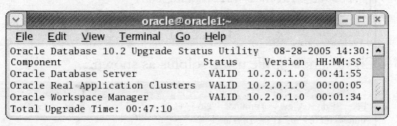

```
oracle@oracle1:~                                    _ □ ×
File   Edit   View   Terminal   Go   Help
Oracle Database 10.2 Upgrade Status Utility    08-28-2005 14:30:
Component                            Status    Version    HH:MM:SS
Oracle Database Server               VALID     10.2.0.1.0  00:41:55
Oracle Real Application Clusters     VALID     10.2.0.1.0  00:00:05
Oracle Workspace Manager             VALID     10.2.0.1.0  00:01:34
Total Upgrade Time: 00:47:10
```

8. Run the *update_tns.sh* script to add the current database into the tnsnames.ora file for the current oracle home. This step must be completed on each node.

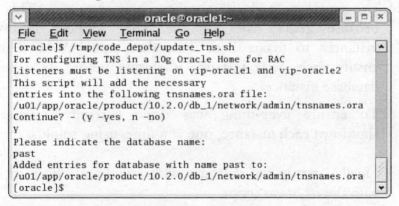

```
oracle@oracle1:~                                    _ □ ×
File   Edit   View   Terminal   Go   Help
[oracle]$ /tmp/code_depot/update_tns.sh
For configuring TNS in a 10g Oracle Home for RAC
Listeners must be listening on vip-oracle1 and vip-oracle2
This script will add the necessary
entries into the following tnsnames.ora file:
/u01/app/oracle/product/10.2.0/db_1/network/admin/tnsnames.ora
Continue? - (y -yes, n -no)
y
Please indicate the database name:
past
Added entries for database with name past to:
/u01/app/oracle/product/10.2.0/db_1/network/admin/tnsnames.ora
[oracle]$
```

9. Edit the file *initpast.ora* to change the parameters shown.

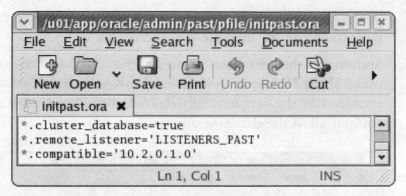

```
*.cluster_database=true
*.remote_listener='LISTENERS_PAST'
*.compatible='10.2.0.1.0'
```

10. Create a new spfile using sqlplus as shown.

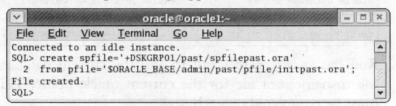

```
Connected to an idle instance.
SQL> create spfile='+DSKGRP01/past/spfilepast.ora'
  2  from pfile='$ORACLE_BASE/admin/past/pfile/initpast.ora';
File created.
SQL>
```

11. Use srvctl to add the database and instances. This time, because PAST relies on the ASM service, modify the instances to make them dependent upon ASM. This will ensure each ASM instance is started before its dependent database instance.

To ensure everything was done correctly, startup and shutdown each instance, one at a time, using sqlplus.

Finally, startup the database with srvctl and check its status with the *crs_status* script.

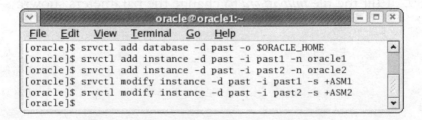

```
[oracle]$ srvctl add database -d past -o $ORACLE_HOME
[oracle]$ srvctl add instance -d past -i past1 -n oracle1
[oracle]$ srvctl add instance -d past -i past2 -n oracle2
[oracle]$ srvctl modify instance -d past -i past1 -s +ASM1
[oracle]$ srvctl modify instance -d past -i past2 -s +ASM2
[oracle]$
```

The asmcmd Utility

A new command line tool is included with 10g release 2 called *asmcmd*. Figure 11.3 shows that it is launched by first setting the environment for +ASM, then calling it with the asmcmd command. The idea of this tool is to make administering the asm files similar to administering standard operating system files.

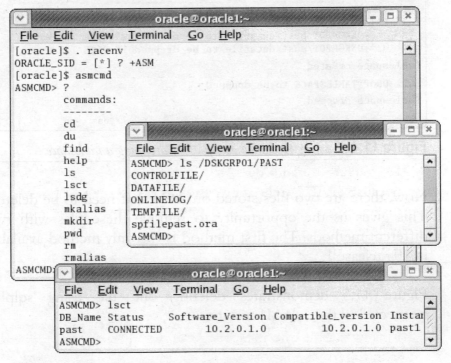

Figure 11.3: *Trying out the asmcmd utility.*

Two Methods for Deleting Orphaned ASM Files

The *asmcmd* is a great tool for deleting orphaned files; files left over from previously dropped tablespaces. We have learned that if a datafile is created using only the diskgroup name, it will be automatically deleted if the tablespace is dropped. However, if a datafile is explicitly named, and its tablespace is dropped, it will become orphaned, taking up unnecessary space with no purpose.

Figure 11.4 demonstrates creating a new tablespace with two named datafiles and then dropping it.

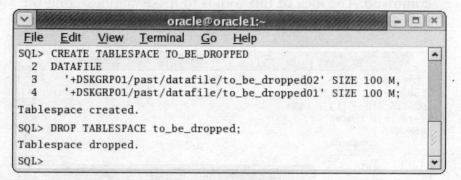

Figure 11.4: *Leaving orphaned datafiles by dropping a tablesapce.*

Now, there are two files stored on ASM that need to be deleted. This gives us the opportunity to remove these files with two different methods. The first method is the only method available in 10g release 1.

Figure 11.5 demonstrates deleting one file using sqlplus connected to the +ASM1 instance.

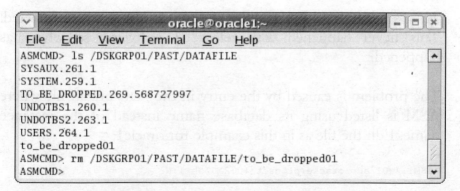

```
oracle@oracle1:~
File   Edit   View   Terminal   Go   Help
SQL> select    name,
  2            file_number,
  3            file_incarnation
  4     from v$asm_alias
  5     where upper(name) like 'TO_BE_DROPPED%';
NAME                              FILE_NUMBER FILE_INCARNATION
-----------------------------     ----------- ----------------
TO_BE_DROPPED.268.568727979            268          568727979
to_be_dropped02                        268          568727979
TO_BE_DROPPED.269.568727997            269          568727997
to_be_dropped01                        269          568727997
SQL> alter diskgroup DSKGRP01 drop file
  2     '+DSKGRP01.268.568727979';
Diskgroup altered.
SQL>
```

Figure 11.5: *Deleting an orphaned file from the ASM instance.*

Figure 11.6 demonstrates deleting a file using *asmcmd*. Of course, this method is only available after 10g release 2 software is installed.

```
oracle@oracle1:~
File   Edit   View   Terminal   Go   Help
ASMCMD> ls /DSKGRP01/PAST/DATAFILE
SYSAUX.261.1
SYSTEM.259.1
TO_BE_DROPPED.269.568727997
UNDOTBS1.260.1
UNDOTBS2.263.1
USERS.264.1
to_be_dropped01
ASMCMD> rm /DSKGRP01/PAST/DATAFILE/to_be_dropped01
ASMCMD>
```

Figure 11.6: *Deleting an orphaned file using asmcmd.*

The *asmcmd* utility does not provide a command history with the up-arrow key. With rlwrap installed, this can be fixed by adding the following entry to the ~oracle/.bashrc file:

```
alias asmcmd='rlwrap asmcmd'
```

Creating a Database with Database Configuration Assistant

With the ASM instances running on both nodes, try creating an ASM dependant database with dbca. During this attempt, the message seen in Figure 11.7 will appear.

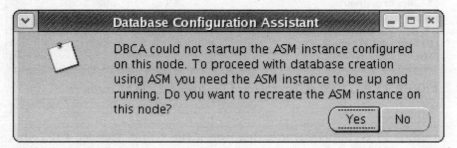

Figure 11.7: *ASM is not detected?*

This is odd. The ASM instance is running but it is not detected! This never happened with release 1 software, so what has happened?

The problem is caused by the entry in the /etc/oratab file where ASM is listed using its database name instead of the instance name. Edit the file as in this example for oracle1:

```
+ASM1:/u01/app/oracle/product/10.2.0/db_1:N
```

Keep in mind that with this change, racenv cannot be used to change the environment to connect to +ASM. Use oraenv instead.

Another consistent problem that has been experienced with the release 2 dbca is the error seen in Figure 11.8.

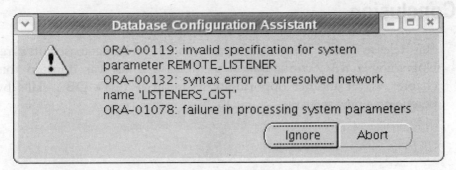

Figure 11.8: *A consistent error with dbca release 2.*

To fix this problem, simply run the *update_tns.sh* script on each node to populate the *tnsnames.ora* in the release 2 home before database creation begins. It is not necessary to restart *dbca* to fix this problem. Click abort and start database creation anew. When the database is finished, edit the tnsnames.ora to check that all service entries are properly written.

An important new feature of *dbca* release 2 is the ability to configure only ASM. In release 1, it had to be done manually or as part of creating a database. This feature can be accessed from the screen depicted in Figure 11.9.

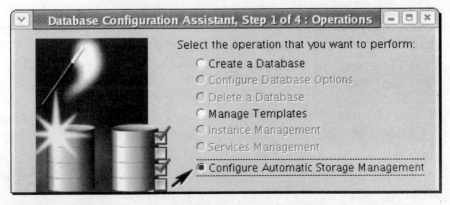

Figure 11.9: *Configuring an ASM instance with dbca.*

Conclusion

10g Release 2 offers many improvements to Oracle database software. Upgrading a RAC configuration to Release 2, as was done in this chapter, is yet another opportunity to improve one's DBA skills by practicing a new scenario.

Linux Commands used in this Project

This book merely touches the surface of the wide range and power of the commands available in Linux. The following table is intended to assist the beginner. All of the commands listed were used at least once while writing this book.

COMMAND	EXAMPLES	WHAT IT DOES
./	./script_to_run	When launching a script from the same directory in which the script is located, it must be preceded by ./ or the operating system will complain that there is no such file.
~/	~/ ~oracle/ ~root/	An abbreviation used to indicate the current user's home directory (~/) or another users home directory.
.	. oraenv . racenv	Period - In the bash shell. A period and space before a script forces the script to run within the shell. This must be done with scripts that export variables into the current shell such as oraenv and racenv.
\	mount /dev/sda11 \ > /mnt/hd	Carry to next line. The slash \ carries the command to the next line.
&	dbca &	Ampersand – used to launch an application as a background process, freeing up the command line for further use.
|	ps –ef | grep ORAC	Pipe – used to send the output from one command into another command.
>	cat 1.log > 2.log cat x.txt >> y.txt cat < 1.log	Redirect – ">" overwrites an existing file, ">>" appends to an existing file. "<" redirects as input.

COMMAND	EXAMPLES	WHAT IT DOES
apropos	apropos editor apropos copy apropos search	Searches through the short manual page descriptions for occurrences of the string and display's the results. This command is useful for finding commands that are appropriate for a given task.
cat	cat /path/filename cat file1 file2 > a.txt	Reads a file and prints it to the display. Can be used to combine two or more files into a new file.
cd	cd /etc cd $ORACLE_HOME	Changes to the directory indicated. Typing the cd command by itself changes the user to his home directory.
chkconfig	chkconfig sendmail off chkconfig --list sendmail chkconfig –list	Used to set services to turn on at boot according to run level. It can also be used to list the current settings for a given service or all services.
chgrp	chgrp oinstall filename.txt	Changes the group of a given file.
chmod	chmod 755 /path/filename	Changes the access mode or permissions on the file.
chown	chown oracle:dba /u01 –R chown oracle:dba filename	Changes ownership of a file to owner:group. The –R switch makes the command recursive, applying changes to all files in subdirectories.
cp	cp /etc/hosts /etc/hosts.orig	Makes a copy of a file. Can be used with wildcards to copy more than one file from one directory to another.
dd	dd if=old_file of=new_file dd if /dev/zero of=file count=9	Copies an input file (if) to an output file (of). Use with /dev/zero as input to pre-create binary files for swap space, etc. Use count to indicate the number of blocks to copy. Use bs to indicate the block size.
df	df df –m df –h	Reports the amount of free disk space on mounted file systems. The –m switch reports in megabytes. The –h switch makes the output human friendly (mix of megabytes and gigabytes).
dmesg	dmesg dmesg |grep ERROR –B5	Prints the boot messages to screen. Use with the grep command to reduce the output.
e2fsck	e2fsck /dev/hda1	Runs a file system check on an unmounted file system.

COMMAND	EXAMPLES	WHAT IT DOES
echo	echo $PS1 echo $ORACLE_HOME	Returns the value for a given shell variable.
eject	eject /mnt/cdrom	Used to eject a cdrom that is not mounted.
env	env | grep ORACLE	Returns only environmental variables.
exit	exit	Exits the current terminal window, session or job.
export	export $ORACLE_SID=+ASM `export PATH=$PATH:/sbin`	Sets the value of a variable and makes it available to all processes that belong to the current shell.
grep	grep searchstring filename grep –A3 –B3 string file	Searches though the lines of a text file or input and limits its output to only those lines that contain the searchstring. The –Bx and –Ax switches request grep to include a number of lines before and after the match, where x is the number of lines to include.
`groupadd`	`groupadd dba`	Adds an operating system group.
history	history history | grep mount	Returns a list of recently used commands. Combine it with grep to find specific commands.
hostname	Hostname	Displays the node's host name.
id	id id oracle	Displays information about a user. If no user is indicated, it displays information about the current login.
ifconfig	/sbin/ifconfig /sbin/ifconfig eth0	Used by root to determine the configuration of the nic cards. Reports the MAC address, IP address, etc. Can be used to configure additional IPs on existing NICs to support VIP service for 10g RAC.
init	init 0 /sbin/init 6	Used by the root user to shutdown or reboot. Changes the runlevel to 0 (shutdown) or 6 (reboot).
less	less /path/filename	Displays the contents of a file to the screen. Scrollable up and down. Type q to exit.

COMMAND	EXAMPLES	WHAT IT DOES
ln	ln /tmp/source /u01/newlink ln –s /tmp/source /u01/link	Creates a second notation on the file system for referring to a given file, essentially a second name for the file. If the original file is deleted, the file is still available through the new name. Use the –s switch to create a symbolic link. When using a symbolic link, if the original file is deleted, the sybolic link becomes broken.
ls	ls –l ls –a ls –la	Lists directory contents. The –l switch displays permissions, ownership, modification time. The –a switch displays all files including hidden files.
man	man grep man which man export –w	Displays the manual pages for a given command. The –w switch displays the file location of the given manual page. Type q to exit a man page.
mkdir	mkdir /new mkdir /new/new/new -p	Makes a directory. The –p switch creates parent directories if they do not exist.
mkfs	mkfs –t ext3 /dev/sda5	Makes a file system on an unmounted partition, useful for wiping out data on a previously used partition.
more	more /path/filename	Displays a file to the screen, one screen amount at a time.
mount	mount /mnt/cdrom mount /dev/hdc1 /u03	Mounts a file system.
mv	mv ~/c.txt /tmp/c.txt mv oldname newname	Moves a file or renames a file.
passwd	passwd oracle	Changes an OS user password.
pkill	pkill oracm	Used to kill a running process.
ps	ps –ef ps -ef | grep oracm	Lists running processes. Useful for tracking who owns a given process. Can be combined with grep to reduce the output to one or a few processes.
pstree	pstree	Displays running processes in a tree format showing the processes that have been launched by other processes as branches of a tree.

COMMAND	EXAMPLES	WHAT IT DOES
pwd	pwd	"Print working directory." Displays the full path to the current working directory.
raw	raw /dev/raw/raw1 /dev/sda1 raw –q /dev/raw/raw1 raw –qa	Binds a raw device to a partition. The switch -q queries, listing a particular raw device. The switch -qa queries all.
rpm	rpm –q ocfs-tools rpm –ql ocfs-tools rpm –ivh emacs-21.3-7 rpm –e emacs-21.3-7	Redhat Package Manager. Used to find what packages are installed, and used to install and uninstall packages. The –q switch queries. The –ql switch lists all associated files. The –ivh switch installs. The –e switch uninstalls.
service	service vsftpd start	Used by root to start and stop services such as ftp.
set	set | grep ORACLE	Returns all variables.
sh	sh script_name	Invokes Bash to run a script.
su	su su oracle	su to switch user. su with no user switches to root. Root can assume another user's identity without a password.
sysctl	sysctl -p	After updating the sysctl.conf file, this command is issued to load the new parameters without having to reboot.
tail	tail filename	Used to read the last 10 lines of a file. A great tool for viewing the last events of a log file.
top	top	Lists the processes ranked by their usage of system resources. This is especially useful to determine if an Oracle program such as dbca is hanging because there will be very little cpu consumption. Type q to quit.
touch	touch filename	Used to update the access and modification times to the current system time. Can also be used to create a new file of zero bytes.
umask	umask –S u=rwx,g=rx,o=rx	Sets the default file permission for files created in this shell or programs launched from it.
umount	umount /mnt/cdrom	Unmounts a mounted file system.
uname	uname –a uname -r	Prints information about the operating system such as the kernel release, date and time of last kernel compile.

COMMAND	EXAMPLES	WHAT IT DOES
unset	unset ORACLE_HOME	Used to remove a variable.
useradd	useradd -g dba fred	Adds a user to the operating system.
usermod	usermod -G oinstall fred	Modifies an operating system user account.
wget	wget www.web.com/script.sh	A non-interactive file download utility that supports http, https, and ftp.
which	which fdisk which gcc	Searches the user's $PATH environment variable to reveal the full path of the file that would be executed if that command were run.
whoami	whoami	This is the Linux equivalent of Oracle's "select user from dual".

Table A.1: *Commands used at least once while writing this book.*

Code Depot

The code depot for this book includes code and images that will make creating and maintaining RAC databases easier. It also includes Oracle Patch 3006854 and the modutils rpm software.

Obtaining the Code_depot.zip file is easy. Figure B.1 demonstrates the wget and unzip commands used to obtain and decompress the file. Switch to the /tmp directory and then use wget to retrieve the file.

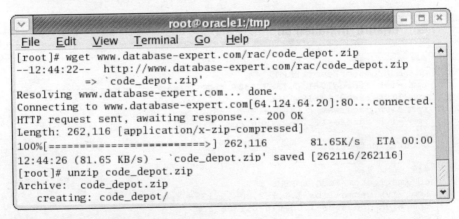

Figure B.1: *Obtaining the code depot.*

README.TXT

This file lists and notes the files that are included. Any additions or changes made after this book is published will be noted in this file.

install_desktop_images.sh

Run *install_desktop_images.sh* script with the command sh *install_desktop_images.sh* to install the desktop image for nodes oracle1 and oracle2. The script will prompt the user for the node number.

ensure_installed.sh

The *ensure_installed.sh* script will verify that all the necessary Linux packages required by Oracle and necessary for this book have been installed. Run it with the command sh *ensure_install.sh*.

The *ensure_installed.sh* script runs the following commands:

💾 **ensure_installed.sh**

```
### CD 1 ###
cd /mnt/cdrom/Fedora/RPMS
rpm -ivh libpng10-1.0.13-9.i386.rpm
rpm -ivh rsh-0.17-19.i386.rpm
rpm -ivh cdda2wav-2.01-0.a19.2.i386.rpm
rpm -ivh cdrdao-1.1.7-7.i386.rpm
cd
umount /mnt/cdrom

### CD 2 ###
cd /mnt/cdrom/Fedora/RPMS
rpm -ivh gnome-libs-1.4.1.2.90-35.i386.rpm
rpm -ivh gtoaster-1.0beta6-6.i386.rpm
cd
umount /mnt/cdrom

### CD 3 ###
cd /mnt/cdrom/Fedora/RPMS
rpm -ivh rsh-server-0.17-19.i386.rpm
rpm -ivh compat-libstdc++-7.3-2.96.118.i386.rpm
rpm -ivh compat-libstdc++-devel-7.3-2.96.118.i386.rpm
rpm -ivh compat-db-4.0.14-2.i386.rpm
rpm -ivh compat-gcc-7.3-2.96.118.i386.rpm
rpm -ivh compat-gcc-c++-7.3-2.96.118.i386.rpm
rpm -ivh sysstat-4.0.7-5.i386.rpm
rpm -ivh openmotif21-2.1.30-8.i386.rpm
rpm -ivh pdksh-5.2.14-23.i386.rpm
rpm -ivh ncurses4-5.0-12.i386.rpm
rpm -ivh libaio-0.3.93-4.i386.rpm
```

```
rpm -ivh libaio-devel-0.3.93-4.i386.rpm
cd
umount /mnt/cdrom
```

os_prep.sh

The *os_prep.sh* script should be run one time only, as root, on each node. It will add the necessary entries into the system configuration files and will also add the following entries into each of the following files:

/etc/modules.conf

```
options sbp2 sbp2_exclusive_login=0
post-install sbp2 insmod sd_mod
post-remove sbp2tmmod sd_mod
```

/etc/sysctl.conf

```
kernel.shmmax=2147483648
kernel.sem=250 32000 100 128
fs.file-max=65536
net.core.rmem_default=262144
net.core.wmem_default=262144
net.core.rmem_max=262144
net.core.wmem_max=262144
```

Oracle Patch 3006854

Refer to the end of Chapter 4 for installation instructions. If the code depot is unavailable, this file can be obtained from http://metalink.oracle.com.

oracle

The "oracle" script is used to ensure that oracle processes start at boot time. Follow the instructions at the end of Chapter 6 to install this script. If the code depot is unavailable, use the following version:

```
### ORACLE Services Startup/Shutdown Script
### Starts and Stops Oracle Services
# chkconfig: 2345 99 1
# description: Starts Oracle 9i Services

# $PATH is required to find oraenv and dbhome
PATH=$PATH:/usr/local/bin
ORAENV_ASK=NO
ORACLE_SID=*
. oraenv

case "$1" in
'start')
    ulimit -u 16384

    ### Load the hangcheck-timer with parameters
    /sbin/rmmod hancheck-timer
    /sbin/insmod hangcheck-timer hangcheck_tick=30
hangcheck_margin=180

    ### Start the Oracle Cluster Manager
    rm -rf $ORACLE_HOME/oracm/log/*.ts
    $ORACLE_HOME/oracm/bin/ocmstart.sh

    ### Start the Listener and Global Services Daemon
    /bin/su - oracle -c "$ORACLE_HOME/bin/lsnrctl start"
    /bin/su - oracle -c "$ORACLE_HOME/bin/gsdctl start"

    ### In a non-rac 9i install, dbstart would be called
    ### to start a database (marked 'Y' in /etc/oratab)
    ### on boot.
    ### /bin/su - oracle -c "$ORACLE_HOME/bin/dbstart"

    ### touch creates a file that asks system to
    ### stop Oracle when system shuts down
    ### Do not use; Allow the system to kill oracle services
    ### or there will be errors at shutdown
    ### touch /var/lock/subsys/oracle
    ;;
'stop')
    /bin/su - oracle -c "$ORACLE_HOME/bin/gsdctl stop"
    /bin/su - oracle -c "$ORACLE_HOME/bin/lsnrctl stop"
    ;;
esac
```

install_scripts.sh

This script, when run as root, will copy the racenv and *crs_status* scripts into the /usr/local/bin directory and set the necessary permissions for these files.

racenv

The oraenv script used to set environmental variables is beneficial when running Oracle in a non-clustered environment. The code depot for this book includes a script called racenv, which is a modified version of the oraenv script. Use the racenv script to set the variables in a RAC environment.

To use the racenv script, issue the command . racenv. The racenv script will ask for one additional item besides the ORACLE_SID, namely the ORACLE_NODE. Accept default values by pressing [enter] with no response. Once racenv has received a value for ORACLE_NODE (a single digit numeric string), it will set a new variable $ORACLE_NODE, and subsequently will not ask for ORACLE_NODE again.

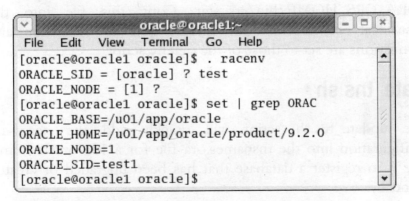

```
oracle@oracle1:~
File   Edit   View   Terminal   Go   Help
[oracle@oracle1 oracle]$ . racenv
ORACLE_SID = [oracle] ? test
ORACLE_NODE = [1] ?
[oracle@oracle1 oracle]$ set | grep ORAC
ORACLE_BASE=/u01/app/oracle
ORACLE_HOME=/u01/app/oracle/product/9.2.0
ORACLE_NODE=1
ORACLE_SID=test1
[oracle@oracle1 oracle]$
```

Figure B.1: *Using the racenv script.*

Racenv is especially useful because it combines the sid with the node number, necessary in a RAC environment. This makes switching between two RAC databases extremely easy, even if those databases are running on different versions of Oracle software.

To use . racenv as a command in a script so that no interaction is required, three variables must be set as follows:

```
ORACLE_SID=sid         # use * for a null sid
ORACLE_NODE=node       # (node must be an integer 1-9)
RACENV_ASK=NO
```

To use racenv in a startup script, set the $PATH variable before using the . racenv command. This will allow the script to find racenv and dbhome. For example:

```
PATH=$PATH:/usr/local/bin
```

crs_status

The *crs_status* script is used to check the status of the services that are run by CRS. It simply reformats the output of $ORA_CRS_HOME/bin/crs_stat. Copy this file into the /usr/local/bin directory and ensure that its ownership and permissions are set to those of the oraenv script.

update_tns.sh

The update_tns.sh script will quickly add the necessary configuration into the tnsnames.ora file for a 10g oracle home. Use it to register a database that has been upgraded or created manually.

Errors, Errors, *Errors!*

A considerable difficulty with Oracle software, or most any software, is the messages that accompany errors can set the administrator off on a wild goose chase. Most messages fail to give a clear indication of what is causing the problem.

This appendix will catalog the various errors encountered while writing this book. It will attempt to explain what caused the error, and explain what was done to solve the problem. The list of errors is presented in roughly the same order as the chapters of this book.

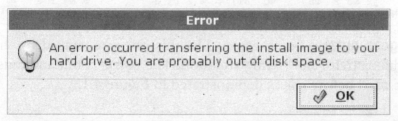

Linux Errors on Install – Errors encountered when installing Fedora, such as the one shown here, can be avoided. On boot, type F2 to enter the options screen, then type linux noprobe <enter>.

```
Kernel panic: Attempted to kill init!
```

Kernel panic: - *This error sounds rather frightening!* It occurs when the gcc compiler fails during the installation of Oracle patch 3006854.

Instead of fixing the problem using the commands demonstrated at the end of Chapter 4, the user himself panics and reboots, only to discover that the kernel has also panicked. To fix this error, boot up with a rescue cd and mount the main system partition. Finally, delete the following file:

```
<mount-point>/etc/ld.so.preload.
```

For instructions on how to use the rescue cd, turn to Appendix D.

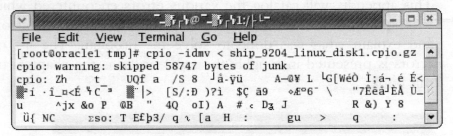

cpio goes nuts! – Some errors, like this one, are caused by the administrator not paying attention. The *gunzip* command must be used before *cpio* as demonstrated in Figure 4.1.

Gnome Toaster Errors – If you launch gtoaster from a system with the modified kernel installed, make sure the external disk is turned on or gtoaster will likely produce this error.

```
[root]# rpm -ivh  ocfs-support-1.0.10-1.i386.rpm
Preparing...          ############################## [100%]
  1:ocfs-support     ############################## [100%]
Checking for Red Hat enterprise kernel: [FAILED]
error: %post(ocfs-support-1.0.10-1) scriptlet failed, exit
[root]# rpm -ivh  ocfs-2.4.21-EL-1.0.14-1.i686.rpm
Preparing...          ############################## [100%]
  1:ocfs-2.4.21-EL  ############################## [100%]
Checking for Red Hat enterprise kernel: [FAILED]
error: %post(ocfs-2.4.21-EL-1.0.14-1) scriptlet failed, exi
```

Checking for Red Hat enterprise kernel [FAILED] – These errors will occur if you try to install OCFS before installing the modified kernel for firewire. Uninstall these packages with the command *rpm -e* and then install the modified kernel.

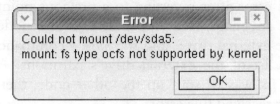

OCFS not supported by kernel - This error occurs when attempting to mount an OCFS file system before OCFS has been loaded. To fix this problem, exit OCFS Tools and run the command *load_ocfs* as root.

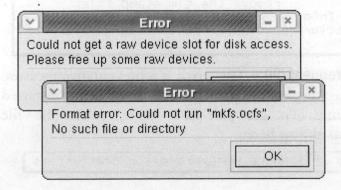

Various ocfstool errors – The ocfstool must be run from an X-windows session, such as gnome, logged in as root. Using the *su* command will create errors because the $PATH variable will not be properly set.

```
Mounting other file systems:
  mount: /dev/sda5 is not a valid block device
  mount: /dev/sda6 is not a valid block device
```

mount: /dev/sda5 is not a valid block device – This error occurs when booting. First, make sure the external drive is turned on. If it is not on, turn it on and reboot both nodes.

During the writing of this book, one of the nodes (oracle2) consistently got this error after reverting to a previous point in the install using an image (see Appendix D). The node could not detect the external drive, and the *fdisk -l* command would not return a list of the external drive's partitions. A quick and sure fire fix was to start up the other node, then reboot the node that received this error.

```
[root]# $ORACLE_HOME/oracm/bin/ocmstart.sh
ocmstart.sh: Error: Restart is too frequent
ocmstart.sh: Info:  Check the system configuration
                    and fix the problem.
ocmstart.sh: Info:  After you fixed the problem,
                    remove the timestamp file
ocmstart.sh: Info:
"/u01/app/oracle/product/9.2.0/oracm/log/ocmstart.ts"
[root]#
```

Restart is too frequent (9i) – This error is a preventative measure by Oracle to keeps the oracm process from being restarted too frequently. To get past this error, delete the file ocmstart.ts as shown here:

```
[root]# rm -f $ORACLE_HOME/oracm/log/ocmstart.ts
```

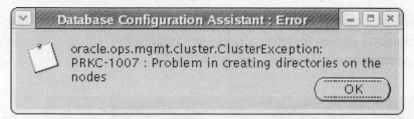

PRKC-1007 (9i) - This error occurs when the dbca is launched after the *su* command. In other words, the dbca is being run as root. Quit the dbca and restart it as oracle.

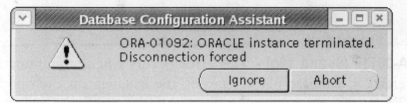

ORA-01092 (9i) – A previous attempt to create a database has failed. This error occurred on the second attempt to create a database. Reboot the node on which the dbca is being run.

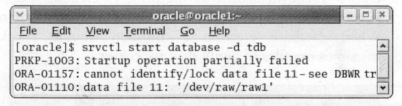

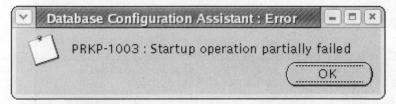

PRKP-1003 – This error means that srvctl cannot start both instances after they are created. Likely, one of the two instances cannot access all of the associated files. Verify that the files are created in directories owned by the oracle user and that the directories can be written to and from each node.

When using raw partitions, ensure that each raw device is bound to its partition and the ownership of the device is correctly set to oracle:oinstall.

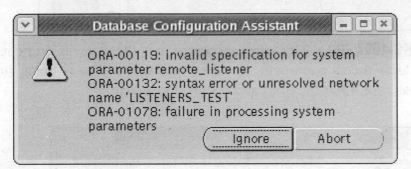

Database Configuration Assistant

ORA-00119: invalid specification for system parameter remote_listener
ORA-00132: syntax error or unresolved network name 'LISTENERS_TEST'
ORA-01078: failure in processing system parameters

Ignore   Abort

ORA-00119 (9i and 10g) - This error occurs when attempting to create a database before starting the listeners on each node. To fix this error, stop the dbca program, configure and start the listeners, then start the dbca process over again.

With 10g Release 2, this error will occur unless you add entries to the tnsnames.ora file prior to creating a database. Run the script update_tns.sh (code depot) on both nodes. When database creation is finished double check the tnsnames.ora files to verify they are correct.

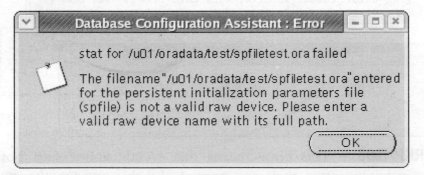

Database Configuration Assistant : Error

stat for /u01/oradata/test/spfiletest.ora failed

The filename "/u01/oradata/test/spfiletest.ora" entered for the persistent initialization parameters file (spfile) is not a valid raw device. Please enter a valid raw device name with its full path.

OK

Stat for spfile failed (9i) – The spfile needs to be stored on a shared device such as the external drive. This error occurs when the spfile is found in a location that is not in shared storage. Unfortunately, this message, which indicates the problem is with raw, is displayed even when using OCFS.

To fix this error, relaunch the dbca with the "-datafileDestination" parameter.

If the dbca was launched with the "-datafileDestination" parameter, check the file system permissions to ensure the oracle user can write to that directory from each node. Ensure the directory is pre-created and is owned by oracle:oinstall.

```
[oracle@oracle1 oracle]$ gsdctl start
Failed to start GSD on local node
[oracle@oracle1 oracle]$
```

Failed to start GSD on local node (9i) - This error occurs when Oracle 9i is installed without pre-creating the directory /var/opt/oracle. This can be fixed after the install. First, create the directory, then create a text file called srvConfig.loc which contains the following text:

```
srvconfig_loc=/u02/oradata/config/9.2.0/srvctlConfig.dbf
```

Ensure all users have read access to the /var/opt/oracle/srvConfig.loc file.

```
[oracle@oracle1 oracle]$ srvctl status database -d test
PRKR-1007 : getting of cluster database test configuration
PRKC-1019 : Error creating handle to daemon on the node or
PRKO-2005 : Application error: Failure in getting Cluster
[oracle@oracle1 oracle]$
```

PRKR-1007 (9i) – This error occurs when attempting to use one of the *srvctl* commands when the global services daemon is not running. Start GSD with the command *gsdctl start*.

```
[oracle]$ srvctl start database -d test
PRKP-1040 : Failed to get status of the listeners
  associated with instance test1 on nodeoracle1
PRKR-1007 : getting of cluster database test
  configuration failed,
PRKC-1018 : Error getting coordinator node
[oracle]$
```

PRKP-1040 (9i) – This error would kill the global services daemon on oracle1 making it difficult to determine if the problem was with gsd or srvctl. A fix is to restart gsd, remove the database from the srvctl repository and then add it back in as follows:

```
[oracle]$ srvctl remove database -d test
Please confirm removal of the database test (y/[n]) y
[oracle]$ srvctl add database -d test -o $ORACLE_HOME
[oracle]$ srvctl add instance -d test -i test1 -n oracle1
[oracle]$ srvctl add instance -d test -i test2 -n oracle2
[oracle]$ srvctl start database -d test
[oracle]$
```

```
[oracle@oracle2 oracle]$ gsdctl stat
CMCLI ERROR: OpenCommPort: connect failed with error 111.
CMCLI ERROR: OpenCommPort: connect failed with error 111.
CMCLI ERROR: OpenCommPort: connect failed with error 111.
PRKC-1021 : Problem in the clusterware
Failed to get list of active nodes from clusterware
[oracle@oracle2 oracle]$
```

CMCLI ERROR (9i) – This error occurs when attempting to use gsdctl without the oracm process running. To fix this error, start oracm as root.

```
[oracle]$ srvctl add database -d test -o $ORACLE_HOME
PRKR-1005 : adding of cluster database test
    configuration failed
PRKR-1064 : General Exception in OCR
```

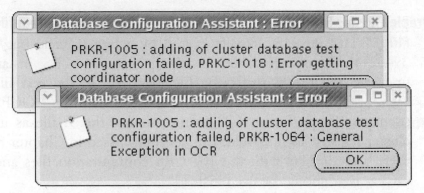

Variations of PRKR-1005 (9i) – These errors occur when the srvctlConfig.dbf file is from a previous install. To fix this error, first delete the file and rebuild it as shown here:

```
[oracle]$ gsdctl stop  ### this command on all nodes!
Successfully stopped GSD on local node
[oracle]$ rm –f /u02/oradata/config/9.2.0/srvctlConfig.dbf
[oracle]$ dd if=/dev/zero \
>  of=/u02/oradata/config/9.2.0/srvctlConfig.dbf \
> bs=1M count=100
100+0 records in
100+0 records out
[oracle]$ srvconfig –init
[oracle]$ gsdctl start ### this command on all nodes!
Successfully started GSD on local node
[oracle]$
```

Keep in mind that recreating the srvctlConfig.dbf file will remove the configuration for all databases. It is necessary to add each pre-existing database back in with srvctl.

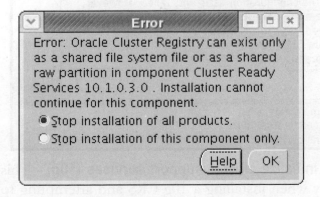

Oracle Cluster Registry can exist only as a shared file system file (10g) - This error is actually caused by a bug (Oracle bug# 3940214). It occurs when installing the 10g CRS in an upgrade, and the 9i srvConfig file identified in the text file /var/opt/oracle/srvConfig.loc, is stored on an OCFS partition. The software will attempt to use the 9i file as its cluster registry, as it should. But, as is discussed in Chapter 8, there are conflicts with the 10g CRS configuration files and OCFS. Raw should be used instead.

If you must store your 10g CRS configuration files on OCFS instead of raw, then there is a "fix" for this bug. Before the 10g CRS install, rename the file /var/opt/oracle/srvConfig.loc to some other name. When the screen "Cluster Node Selection" appears in the install program, rename the file back to its original name. Finally, just before running the $ORA_CRS_HOME/root.sh script, edit the script on both nodes to ensure the file identified on line 212 is the correct path and file name for the 9i configuration file, for example:

```
CRS_OCR_LOCATION=/u02/oradata/config/9.2.0/srvctlConfig.dbf
```

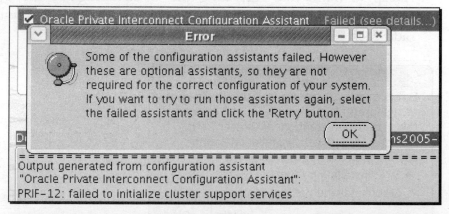

PRIF-12: failed to initialize cluster support services (10g) - This occurs regularly when installing a 10g CRS and attempting to store the configuration files on OCFS. Avoid this problem and other instabilities by saving the CRS configuration and CSS voting files on raw partitions. After this error, the CSS daemon will not start.

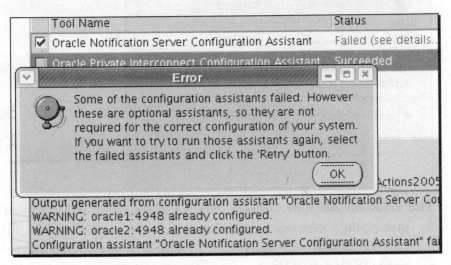

Warning: oracle1:4948 already configured(10g) - This error occurs when installing the 10g CRS configuration files on raw partitions used for a previous 10g install. Avoid this error and other potential problems by overwriting any data on those partitions with the command dd $if=/dev/zero$ $of=/dev/raw/rawX$ before the install.

```
INIT: Id "hx" respawning too fast
    : disabled for 5 minutes
```

Respawning too fast (10g) - One of the 10g CRS services is not able to load and is attempting to respawn. To determine which service is failing, use the command $tail /etc/inittab -n3$ to read the last lines of the inittab file. Match the id to the failing service. Check the log files of the service that is failing.

This error appears regularly on boot when using OCFS to store the CRS config file. The only fix I have found, besides using raw for the CRS file, was to reboot.

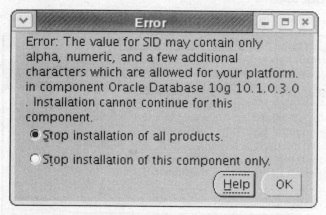

The value for SID may contain only... (10g) - If this error appears, quit the installer and remove the $ORACLE_SID environmental variable with the command *unset ORACLE_SID*......

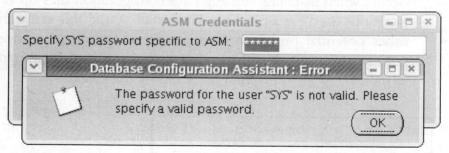

ASM Credentials (10g) - The sys password is invalid. To fix this error, exit the dbca and stop the ASM instances on each node. Create a new password file with the 10g version of orapwd. Ensure the symbolic links to the password file exist in the $ORACLE_HOME/dbs directory of each node. Start the ASM instances and then start the dbca.

Starting GSD hangs during install (10g) – This is a very frustrating error. After working to get a successful install, gsd hangs at 65%! To solve it, run the command *$ORACLE(10g)_HOME/bin/gsdctl stat* on each node. You will likely find that on one node (oracle2) GSD has not started and will not start. Attempting to start it from the command line hangs. Reboot the oracle2 node by running the command */sbin/init 6* as root. The following message will appear on oracle1:

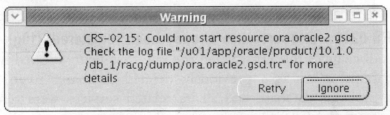

When oracle2 has finished its reboot, click the Retry button. Now you can continue with the install just as if nothing happened. Alternatively, it is possible to run the vipca as root after a reboot of both nodes. The install will still be complete. *Do not forget to run the $ORACLE_HOME/root.sh script on oracle2!*

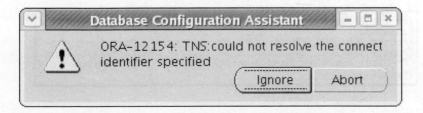

ORA-12154 (10g) - The dbca for Oracle 10g requires the administrator to enter a password for the sys account *before* the database is created. This error occurs when the password includes the symbol "@".

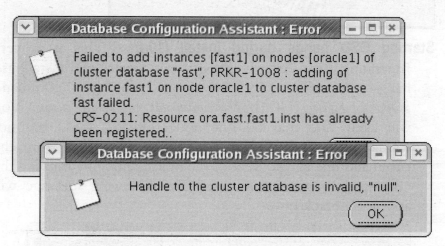

CRS-0211 – Resource has already been registered. (10g) – The dbca gives this error when the database being created has the same name as a previously deleted database. Even if the previous database and all its related services were removed from the CRS file with srvctl, this error can occur. It is not necessary to quit the dbca. Write down the name of the resource that must be removed. Click OK and the second error appears. That is not a problem either. Now open a new terminal and switch to root. Follow the example below to unregister the resource that had been detected as shown below. Then simply continue with the dbca.

```
[oracle]$ su
Password:
[root]# $ORA_CRS_HOME/bin/crs_unregister ora.fast.fast1.inst
[root]# $ORA_CRS_HOME/bin/crs_unregister ora.fast.fast2.inst
CRS-0210: Could not find resource ora.fast.fast2.inst.
[root]#
```

Note that the failure of one *crs_unregister* command implies that the previous removal with srvctl worked for one of the instances but not the other.

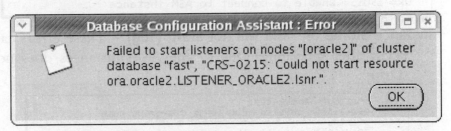

Failed to start listeners (10g) – This error occurs when there is a typo in the /etc/hosts file for one of the VIP entries. Fix this error by first fixing the typo in /etc/hosts. Next, refer to Appendix G to rebuild the CRS file from scratch. *Avoid this error by creating the /etc/hosts files with care!*

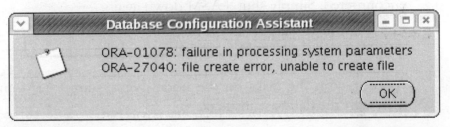

ORA-01078 (10g) - When creating the spfile for an ASM instance on OCFS, this error will occur if the directory it is to be stored in is not pre-created. To fix this error, just open another terminal, create the directory, click OK and try again. The dbca does not have to be restarted. This may be the only case in 10g software where a directory must be pre-created.

```
[oracle]$ srvctl start instance -d last -i last2
PRKP-1001 : Error starting instance last2 on node oracle2
... :SQL> ORA-01078: failure in processing system parameters
... :SQL> Disconnected.
oracle2:ora.last.last2.inst:
CRS-0215: Could not start resource ora.last.last2.inst.
[oracle]$
```

```
SQL> startup
  ORA-17503: ksfdopn:2 Failed to open
             file +DSKGRP01/past/spfilepast.ora
  ORA-15055: unable to connect to ASM instance
```

Instance stored on ASM will not start! (10g) – These errors can occur after rebooting. One of the ASM instances does not startup.

```
SQL> shutdown immediate;
  ORA-15100: invalid or missing diskgroup name
SQL> startup
  ORA-15032: not all alterations performed
  ORA-15063: diskgroup "DSKGRP01" lacks quorum
             of 2 PST disks; 0 found
```

Using sqlplus, shutdown the +ASM instance on the node with the problem. Starting up the +ASM instance again is not necessary, but if done, the errors seen above will be encountered. Simply shut +ASM down again.

```
[root]# /etc/init.d/oracleasm scandisks
```

As root, scan the disks on the node. Next, start +ASM and then start the database instance.

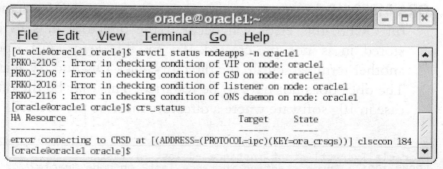

The CRSD will not start on boot! (10g) – Sometimes, this fixes itself with a little patience; however, three minutes is long enough to know that it will not be starting up on its own. This can happen on either node and for no apparent reason.

Use the following commands to stop the CRS service and then restart it. The alternate node should be left alone.

```
[oracle]$ su
Password:
[root]# /etc/init.d/init.crs stop
Shutting down Oracle Cluster Ready Services (CRS):
/etc/init.d/init.crsd: line 188:  4833 Aborted
                       $ORA_CRS_HOME/bin /crsd -2
Shutting down CRS daemon.
Shutting down EVM daemon.
Shutting down CSS daemon.
Shutdown request successfully issued.
[root]# /etc/init.d/init.crs start
Preparing Oracle Cluster Ready Services (CRS):
[root]#
```

Allow at least 2 minutes for the CRS to stop. Even though the *init.crs start* command appears to finish quickly, allow the node a few minutes (sometimes up to 10 minutes!) for the CRS services to spawn.

Note: On my computers, this problem exists with Release 1 only. With Release 2, the CRS starts consistently, but requires a few minutes after boot has completed in order to start.

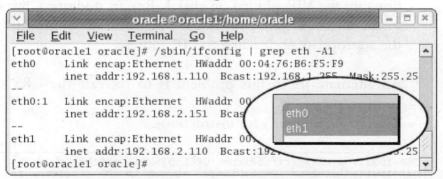

VIP address has been assigned to the wrong NIC! (10g) - Use the *ifconfig* command to show the NIC card that VIP is assigned to. If you find it is on the wrong NIC, you may remember that when running vipca, you allowed for the default action when choosing the NIC, which is, oddly enough, both NICs. Simply clicking "Next" at that point can put the VIP on either NIC. By the way, just because the VIPs start on the right

NICs, does not mean that after reboot they will still be on the right NICs!

There are two possible solutions to this problem. The first one is shown below.

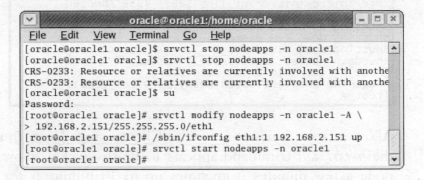

```
oracle@oracle1:/home/oracle
File  Edit  View  Terminal  Go  Help
[oracle@oracle1 oracle]$ srvctl stop nodeapps -n oracle1
[oracle@oracle1 oracle]$ srvctl stop nodeapps -n oracle1
CRS-0233: Resource or relatives are currently involved with anothe
CRS-0233: Resource or relatives are currently involved with anothe
[oracle@oracle1 oracle]$ su
Password:
[root@oracle1 oracle]# srvctl modify nodeapps -n oracle1 -A \
> 192.168.2.151/255.255.255.0/eth1
[root@oracle1 oracle]# /sbin/ifconfig eth1:1 192.168.2.151 up
[root@oracle1 oracle]# srvctl start nodeapps -n oracle1
[root@oracle1 oracle]#
```

Use srvctl to stop the nodeapps services. If this action hangs, use CTL+C to cancel and then stop it again. Ignore the CRS-0233 errors. Next, switch to the root user. Use srvctl to modify the nodeapps configuration. Use ifconfig to manually bring up the VIP address on eht1:1. Restart nodeapps. Switch to the alternate node and run through the same steps using the appropriate node name and IP address.

An alternate fix to this problem is to recreate the CRS file from scratch.

Turn to Appendix G for instructions.

```
ORA-15031: disk specification 'ORCL:DISK01' matches no disks
ORA-15014: location 'ORCL:DISK01' is not in the discovery set
```

ORA-15031 and ORA-15014 (10g) - These errors can occur when attempting to create an ASM disk group from the command line. This error happens when starting up the new ASM instance with an spfile that was created from a pfile that was created by the dbca. Fix it with the following command:

```
SQL> alter system set asm_diskstring='ORCL:*' scope=both;
```

A similar problem can occur when using the dbca. If the member disks do not appear, click the button "Change Disk Discovery Path" and type in ORCL:* as shown below:

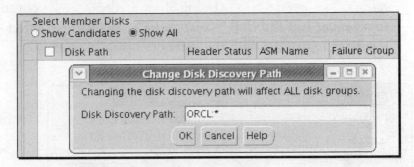

```
[oracle]$ srvctl status database -d test
PRKR-1007 : getting of cluster database test
            configuration failed,
PRKR-1078 : Database test cannot be administered
            using current version of srvconfig.
            Instead run srvconfig from
            /u01/app/oracle/product/9.2.0
PRKO-2005 : Application error
          : Failure in getting Cluster Database
            Configuration for: test
[oracle]$
```

PRKR-1007 (9i and 10g interaction) - This error occurs when attempting to manage a 9i database using the 10g version of srvctl. The 9i version of srvctl is supported by the 10g CRS. However, the 10g srvctl cannot be used to administer a 9i database. Use the racenv script to change the $PATH variable to point to the 9i srvctl.

```
[oracle]$ srvctl start database -d test
PRKP-1040 : Failed to get status of the listeners
    associated with instance test1 on nodeoracle1
[oracle]$ srvctl status database -d test
Instance test1 is running on node oracle1
Instance test2 is running on node oracle2
[oracle]$
```

PRKP-1040 - Failed to get status of listeners (9i and 10g interaction) – This error occurs when starting a 9i RAC database that is being supported by 10g listeners. The database will start successfully even if this error occurs. *Ignore this error!* Using the command *lsnrctl status LISTENER_<node_name>*, check whether the database registered with the listeners upon startup.

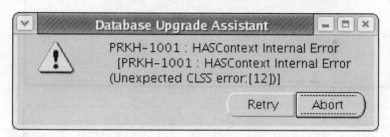

PRKH-1001 – This error occurs when using the database upgrade assistant. Avoid this error by editing the dbua script so that the LD_LIBRARY_PATH variable definition on line 135 begins with the path */etc/ORCLcluster/oracm/lib*.

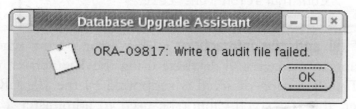

ORA-09817 – Check for available disk space on the drive where the directory $ORACLE_BASE/admin/<database_name> is located.

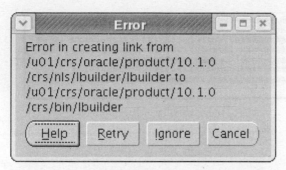

```
Error
Error in creating link from
/u01/crs/oracle/product/10.1.0
/crs/nls/lbuilder/lbuilder to
/u01/crs/oracle/product/10.1.0
/crs/bin/lbuilder

  Help      Retry     Ignore    Cancel
```

Error in creating link (installing Release2 Clusterware) – Avoid this error! Fixing it after the fact requires you to uninstall clusterware. If the installer complains that the preupdate.sh script needs to be run (as seen in the last entry on the "Prerequisite Checks" page), quit the installer and run the script again on each node, even if it was run previously. The preupdate.sh script must complete without intervention.

```
SQL*Plus: Release 10.2.0.1.0 - Production on Sat Aug 27 22:16:40
Copyright (c) 1982, 2005, Oracle.  All rights reserved.
Enter user-name: sys as sysdba
Enter password:
  oracle+ASM2: error while loading shared libraries:
          libaio.so.1: cannot open shared object file:
          No such file or directory
ERROR:
ORA-12547: TNS:lost contact
```

libaio.so.1 cannot open shared object file (10g Release 2) – This will be a common error for many people who install Oracle 10g Release 2. It is *required* that the following packages be installed. Insert the Fedora Install Disk 3 and use the *rpm -ivh* command to install them as root. These packages were not required previously. Technically, a newer version of this software is required (libaio-0.3.96-5 or higher), but this version will fix the problem.

```
[root]# cd /mnt/cdrom/Fedora/RPMS
[root]# rpm -ivh libaio-0.3.93-4.i386.rpm
Preparing...        ################################### [100%]
   1:libaio          ################################### [100%]
[root]# rpm -ivh libaio-devel-0.3.93-4.i386.rpm
Preparing...        ################################### [100%]
   1:libaio-devel    ################################### [100%]
[root]# cd
```

System Rescue and Reverting to an Image

It takes a long time to set up the operating system for a RAC install only to discover on reboot that a typographical error in a configuration is preventing the node from booting. If a problem such as this occurs, it is necessary to boot to a different Linux kernel, mount the disk with the offending configuration file and edit the file.

Chapter 2 covers downloading and burning to CD the software SystemRescueCd freely available at http://www.sysresccd.org/. This software is a bootable Linux kernel which includes a complete set of Linux commands that can be used to rescue a node that will not boot. The CD includes many other programs, most notably Partimage. This program can be used to quickly make a compressed image of a partition and will back up all the work done to configure a node up to that point.

The tricky part of using SystemRescueCd is mounting the right file system. Figure D.1 shows a screenshot of using the command fdisk -l to determine the available hard disk partitions. Take note, the names of partitions such as /dev/hda1 and /dev/hda2 that are used in Fedora are quite different when using SystemRescueCd. As Figure D.1 shows, the first hard drive is called /dev/ide/host0/bus0/target0/lun0/disc and the first partition is called /dev/ide/host0/bus0/target0/lum0/part1.

There are a few mount-points available in the directory /mnt. As an alternative, a new mount-point can be created with the command mkdir /mnt/mount-point-name, using whatever name for the mount-point that is preferred such as /mnt/hd.

Mounting a partition requires a rather lengthy command. The file system type switch is optional:
mount /dev/ide/host0/bus0/target1/lun0/part1 /mnt/hd -t ext3.

```
18:03 root@cdimage /root % fdisk -l
Disk /dev/ide/host0/bus0/target0/lun0/disc: 20.4 GB
16 heads, 63 sectors/track, 39566 cylinders
Units = cylinders of 1008 * 512 = 516096 bytes
                              Device Boot Start    End   Blocks
 Id   System
/dev/ide/host0/bus0/target0/lun0/part1   *     1    203   102280+
 83  Linux
/dev/ide/host0/bus0/target0/lun0/part2       204  37486  18790632
 83  Linux
/dev/ide/host0/bus0/target0/lun0/part3     37487  39566   1048320
 82  Linux swap

Disk /dev/ide/host0/bus0/target1/lun0/disc: 4311 MB
255 heads, 63 sectors/track, 524 cylinders
Units = cylinders of 16065 * 512 = 8225280 bytes
                              Device Boot Start    End   Blocks
 Id   System
/dev/ide/host0/bus0/target1/lun0/part1         1    524   4208998+
 83  Linux
18:03 root@cdimage /root % mkdir /mnt/hd
18:03 root@cdimage /root % mount /dev/ide/host0/bus0/target1/lu
n0/part1 /mnt/hd -t ext3
18:03 root@cdimage /root %
```

Figure D.1: *Mounting a file system from the rescue disk.*

Once a file system is mounted, it is a simple matter to use the vi editor to edit and save a configuration file. A wide range of Linux commands can be used to create, delete, move, compile, change file attributes or do most anything that needs done to fix a problem.

Partimage

The SystemRescueCd includes Partimage, an easy-to-use software for taking an image of a partition. That image can later be used to revert to that point in the configuration. Partimage was used repeatedly in writing this book and is worthy of mention.

The nodes used for writing this book had two internal hard disks installed. On a given node, the hard disk used for installing Fedora and Oracle was the one with the most space, between 10 to 20 gigabytes. The smaller disk was used to store images of the install.

To take an image of a partition, boot to the SystemRescueCd and mount the partition used for storing images as shown in Figure D.1. Do not mount the other partitions. Launch the software with the command partimage.

Follow the steps on the partimage screen. It is a simple matter to determine the partitions to save. The boot partition will be small and its file system will be ext3. The Fedora partition will be large and its file system will be ext3. Take images of both.

Saving an image takes about one minute per 500 megabytes when saving to a partition on a separate physical disk; whereas, saving a partition to a file on the same physical disk will take much longer. The image file of a partition will likely require 10 to 20 percent of the disk space required for the entire partition.

Reverting to a partition is also very simple and much faster than saving. It takes from 5 to 7 minutes to revert to a saved image for a partition of 15 gigabytes when using separate physical disks.

The most desirable points in which to take an image of the system are just before the Oracle 9i software install and just before the install of each Oracle 10g release.

Alternative Linux Windows Managers

When starting Fedora for the very first time, it will launch into the gnome desktop environment, Fedora's default windows manager. One of the best features of Linux is that gnome is not the only graphical interface available. This appendix will demonstrate how to use two alternative windows managers that can be very useful to the Oracle Database Administrator.

Gnome is attractive to the eye and easy to use. However, under certain conditions, such as creating a 10g database, the administrator needs all the CPU and RAM he can get, especially when using old PCs with limited resources.

Changing the Default Run Level

As discussed in Chapter 3, the run level of a Linux computer describes whether the system will boot to a graphical interface (level 5) or a command line (level 3).

It can be very useful to change the run level from 5 to 3. When booting up, instead of a graphical login, a command line login will be seen. All that is needed at that point is the command used to launch the desired windows manager. Quitting a windows manager will bring the user back to the command prompt. Compare that to level 5, in which the only way to change windows managers is to run the command init 3 as root, which will reboot the machine.

To change the default run level, edit the file /etc/inittab and change the line that describes the default run level so it reads:

```
id:3:initdefault:
```

Then, reboot the machine. When the machine finishes rebooting, login at the command prompt, and issue the startx command to launch the gnome interface. To return to the command prompt, logout of gnome.

Trivial Windows Manager (TWM)

The trivial windows manager is the ultimate in lightweight windows managers. Its strength is it has almost no features at all, which means it requires very little of CPU and RAM. About the only things a user will be able to do is to move, minimize and resize various windows.

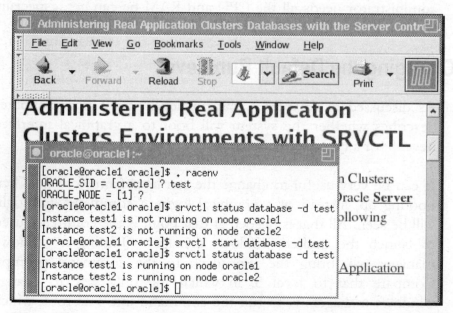

Figure E.1: *The Trivial Windows Manager.*

Use the command xinit /usr/X11R6/bin/twm to launch the trivial windows manager. At first, all that appears is a black screen with an X for the mouse cursor in the middle. Click on the desktop, and the options menu appears. Launch a terminal by selecting xterm. From the terminal, any program can be launched.

🔔 Note – twm is in use does not mean that gnome applications cannot be run. To the contrary, any gui application can be run. So, if gnome-terminal or gedit or mozilla is desired, just launch it from the command prompt. Use the ampersand at the end of the command (such as *gftp &*) to run the process in the background, so as not to tie up the command line.

FVWM

Another windows manager that is worthy of mention is fvwm, a lightweight windows manager with more features than twm. Download fvwm at http://fvwm-themes.sourceforge.net/rpm/. At the bottom of that page is a link to required packages. Click it and download libstroke-0.4-1mdk.i586.rpm. Install the packages in the order shown in Figure E.2.

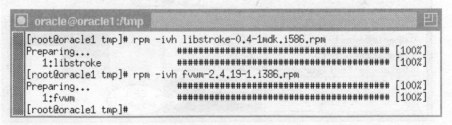

Figure E.2: *Installing fvwm.*

Once fvwm is installed, exit twm and use the command xinit /usr/bin/fvwm to launch fvwm. The initial screen will be very bare. Click the desktop and run the setup form. Select all the available modules and click to copy the config files and restart

---

fvwm. This will create text configuration files in the directory ~/.fvwm for the current user only. These files can be edited to change the fvwm desktop appearance and functionality.

Fvwm can be an excellent desktop manager for installing Oracle software or creating databases. Figure E.3 shows the dbca running in the fvwm window with the CPU monitor below it showing the CPU activity as the database nears completion.

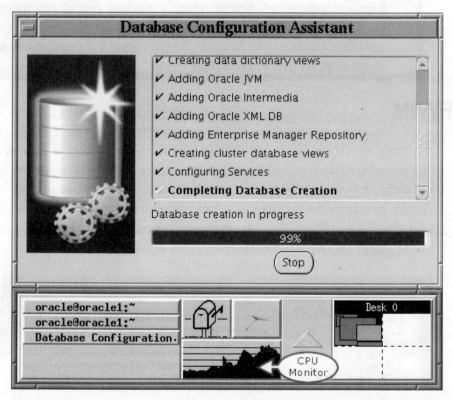

Figure E.3: *Database Configuration Assistant running in fvwm window.*

FVWM's CPU monitor is a fast and easy method to ensure that database creation is not hanging. If the CPU is being utilized, then database creation is still ongoing.

Using the Alias Command to Simplify Launching Windows Managers

To make launching the desired windows manager a simple, easy to remember command, add the following lines to the ~/.bashrc file of each user who desires it:

```
alias fvwm="xinit /usr/bin/fvwm"
alias gnome="xinit /usr/bin/gnome-session"
alias twm="xinit /usr/X11R6/bin/twm"
```

Launching a WM without Tying up the Command Prompt

Use the ampersand at the end of the command to launch a windows manager. By doing so, the terminal login can be returned to by typing [ctl+alt+F1] without having to quit the windows manager to free up the command prompt. To return to the windows manager, type [ctl+alt+F7].

Launching a GUI Program without a Windows Manager

It is possible to launch an Oracle GUI program without being in a windows manager interface. For example, the command xinit $ORACLE_HOME/bin/dbca will launch the database configuration assistant alone with no window around the application. This is not advised because control will be lost over which windows appear on top and whether the windows that appear can be moved or minimized.

Software for the Microsoft Windows Client Machine

There are a number of programs available for download from the internet that can be used to administer an Oracle RAC Database on Linux from a windows machine.

Initial Setup

Oracle's sqlnet cannot always resolve services when static IP addresses are used directly in the tnsnames.ora file. To prevent having to use static IPs in that file, the windows operating system must be configured to resolve the network names where you are expecting to find listeners.

Just as each of the Linux machines has the file /etc/hosts to resolve names to IP addresses on the local network, the windows machine has the file %systemroot%\system32\drivers\etc\hosts. This file can be edited with notepad, placing the name and associated IP address of machines on the internal network as shown in Figure F1.

```
# Copyright (c) 1993-1999 Microsoft Corp.
#
# This file contains the mappings of IP addresses to
# host names. Each entry should be kept on an
# individual line. The IP address should be placed
# in the first column followed by the corresponding
# host name. The IP address and the host name should
# be separated by at least one space.

127.0.0.1         localhost

192.168.2.110     oracle1
192.168.2.120     oracle2
192.168.2.151     vip-oracle1
192.168.2.152     vip-oracle2
```

Figure F.1: *Editing the hosts file of a Microsoft Windows client.*

 Do not be surprised if when opening the hosts file there are entries that were placed there by spyware or other viral software. In most cases, it is a good idea to delete or comment out entries not recognized.

Putty

Putty is a freeware terminal client that supports ssh and telnet, available at http://www.chiark.greenend.org.uk/~sgtatham/putty/. Putty is very easy to use. It supports copying and pasting text with the mouse. It allows the administrator to carry out OS commands and to run sqlplus on the server to connect and administer the database. Fedora has the ssh service turned on by default, and ssh allows root to login, something not supported by telnet. Putty gives the administrator full control of Linux servers from a remote connection.

Oracle Client Software

Oracle offers software that can be downloaded freely from its website (otn.oracle.com) that will enable the user to connect to the database. I suggest downloading the Oracle Database 10g Client for Microsoft Windows (32-bit) which can be found on the database download page. At the time of this publication, only Release 1 is available. Many 3rd party tools such as TOAD or PL/SQL Developer require this full version; they will not function with the "instant client". Install the administrator version (460 MB).

Once the client software is installed, use ftp to get a copy of the tnsnames.ora file from one of the nodes of the RAC. Note: to start the ftp service on a node, as root, run the command /sbin/service vsftpd start. The tnsnames.ora from different versions (9i, 10g) can be appended into one file on the client machine.

TOAD

Originally called Tool for Oracle Application Developers, TOAD is an excellent productivity tool for DBAs and Developers. Trial versions are available for download at http://www.quest.com/.

PL/SQL Developer

PL/SQL Developer is another excellent tool for developing PL/SQL objects. Trial versions are available for download at http://allroundautomations.com/.

VI for Windows

A database administrator on a Linux or UNIX system cannot escape the VI editor. It is also available as a free download for windows at http://www.vim.org/download.php.

Rebuilding 10g CRS Files Without Reinstalling

There are times when CRS files need rebuilt. On a production server this would be rare, but for a student project like this one, things tend to get messy. Not only are many changes made, which invites errors, but there are times in which you will simply want to start over without reinstalling the software.

10g Release 1 Instructions

To begin, switch to the root user and change directories to $ORA_CRS_HOME/install. Run the rootdelete.sh script as shown in Figure G.1. It may appear to hang at a message that reads in part "Aborted" but allow it a couple of minutes to complete. This script should be run from each node.

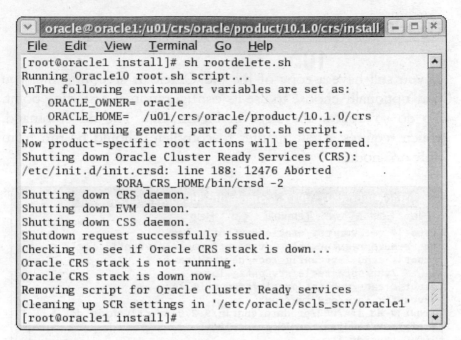

Figure G.1: *Run the rootdelete.sh script.*

Next, run the rootdeinstall.sh script as shown in Figure G.2. Allow this script to finish on one node before beginning it on the next.

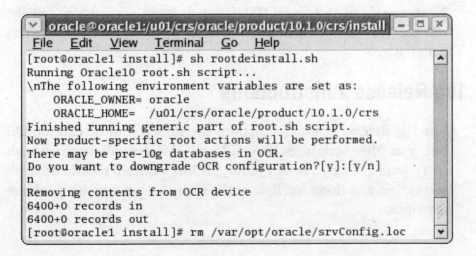

Figure G.2: *Run the rootdeinstall.sh script.*

If you still have a copy of the old Oracle 9i srvconfig file, you may optionally choose to use its configuration as a starting point. To do so, follow the steps in Figure G.3. The dd command, which requires a few minutes to complete, should be run from only one node.

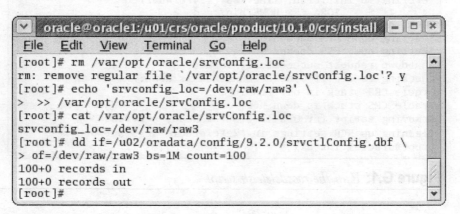

Figure G.3: *Restore the 9i srvConfig file to raw3.*

At this point, run $ORA_CRS_HOME/root.sh from each node. Next, run $ORACLE_HOME/root.sh from each node. Finally, run the 10g version of netca, as oracle, to re-register the listeners with CRS.

10g Release 2 Instructions

For 10g Release 2, the instructions are similar, but be careful. Do not run the scripts $ORA_CRS_HOME/install/rootdelete.sh first and then $ORA_CRS_HOME/install/rootdeinstall.sh second, as was done for Release 1. These scripts cause a problem for vipca.

They make it so that vipca cannot create a new vip, gsd, and ons! Figure G.4 shows the error I have experienced both on the command line and as seen through the vipca tool. The only fix I have found for this error is to revert to an image of Release 1 software, then to reinstall Release 2.

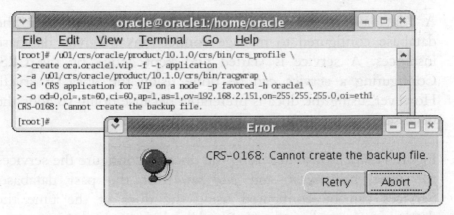

Figure G.4: *Avoid this vipca error!*

To rebuild the 10g Release 2 CRS, run the following scripts. Each script must be completed on each node before continuing to the next script.

```
$ORA_CRS_HOME/release1/rootdelete.sh
$ORA_CRS_HOME/release1/rootdeinstall.sh
$ORA_CRS_HOME/release1/root.sh
$db10g1/root.sh          ### will launch vipca on first node
$db10g2/root.sh
gedit /etc/oratab        ### fix the entry for * to 10g-R2 home
$db10g2/bin/netca        ### run as the oracle user, not root
```

Clearly, this is a hack (the files in the release1 directory were copied from the previous release). Although it works, it is doubtful that Oracle Support would agree with it.

10g Database Services for High Availability

A "database service" is an additional service other than the database configured to manage connections to given database instances. A service is started and kept active by the CRS. Configuring a service can be done using the dbca or srvctl. However, using the dbca is preferable because doing so adds the necessary entries to the tnsnames.ora file.

Figure H.1 demonstrates using the dbca to configure the services *past_forms*, *past_admin*, and *past_rman* for the past database. Services can be configured using the dbca at the time the database is created or after the database is created.

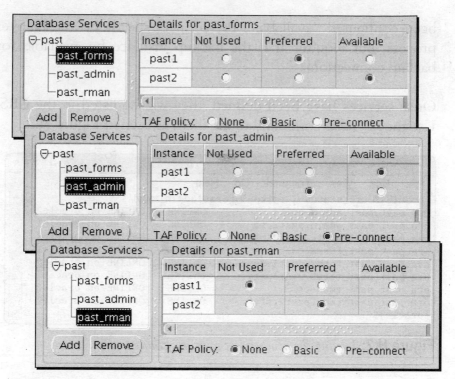

Figure H.1: *Configuring three services using configuration assistant.*

The administrator has planned for the instance past1 to be used for the business forms, and for the instance past2 to be used for administration and rman. The services have been configured so that *past_forms* will prefer past1 but still have access to past2 in the event of a failure on past1. The opposite is true for *past_admin*. The service *past_rman* will only connect to the instance past2.

The TAF (Transparent Application Failover) policy is set in this step as well. The three options are none, basic, and pre-connect. Failover is the concept that if an instance fails, the connection will transfer to an alternate instance. Basic TAF establishes a new connection to an alternate instance when the failure occurs. Pre-connect TAF establishes a second connection to a node that has been configured "available". Pre-connect speeds up the failover process, but requires that the backup instance be available for backup connections.

Once services have been defined, they will be listed in the CRS. Use the *crs_status* command to list them as seen in Figure H.2.

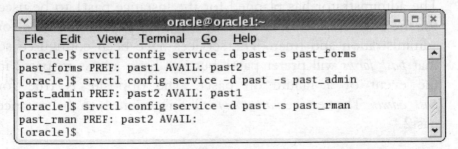

```
oracle@oracle1:~
File   Edit   View   Terminal   Go   Help
[oracle]$ crs_status | egrep  'forms|admin|rman'
ora.past.past_admin.cs               ONLINE    ONLINE on oracle2
ora.past.past_admin.past2.sa         ONLINE    ONLINE on oracle1
ora.past.past_admin.past2.srv        ONLINE    ONLINE on oracle2
ora.past.past_forms.cs               ONLINE    ONLINE on oracle1
ora.past.past_forms.past1.sa         ONLINE    ONLINE on oracle2
ora.past.past_forms.past1.srv        ONLINE    ONLINE on oracle1
ora.past.past_rman.cs                ONLINE    ONLINE on oracle2
ora.past.past_rman.past2.srv         ONLINE    ONLINE on oracle2
[oracle]$
```

Figure H.2: *Listing the new services with crs_status.*

Figure H.3 demonstrates using the srvctl utility to verify and view the configuration of services for the past database.

```
oracle@oracle1:~
File   Edit   View   Terminal   Go   Help
[oracle]$ srvctl config service -d past -s past_forms
past_forms PREF: past1 AVAIL: past2
[oracle]$ srvctl config service -d past -s past_admin
past_admin PREF: past2 AVAIL: past1
[oracle]$ srvctl config service -d past -s past_rman
past_rman PREF: past2 AVAIL:
[oracle]$
```

Figure H.3: *Checking the configuration of services with srvctl.*

Services can also be viewed while connected to the database. Figure H.4 demonstrates listing the connections created in this exercise.

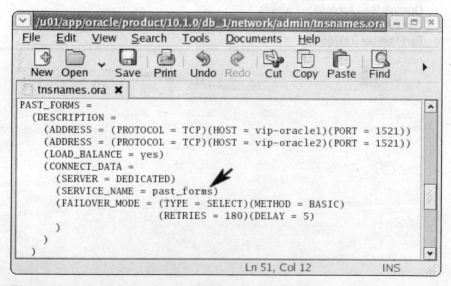

Figure H.4: *Viewing the new services from the database.*

After setting up the services desired with the dbca, open the tnsnames.ora file with a text editor and read through the new entries. Figure H.5 shows the entry for the *past_forms* service just created. Notice that the service name is not the database name.

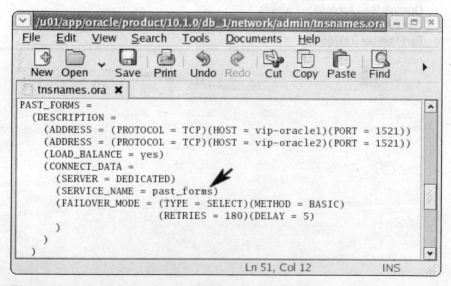

Figure H.5: *The tnsnames.ora entry for past_forms.*

The srvctl utility can be used to add, remove, start and stop services. The following examples demonstrate these functions using srvctl:

```
srvctl add service -d past -s past_forms -r past1 -a past2
srvctl remove service -d past -s past_forms
srvctl start service -d past -s past_forms
srvctl stop service -d -past -s past_forms
```

For more information about configuring services for high availability, visit http://tahiti.oracle.com and search for the following documents:

WITHIN THE DOCUMENT	SEARCJ FOR
Oracle® Database Net Services Reference Guide – Part Number B10776-01	Local Naming Parameters (tnsnames.ora)
Oracle® Real Application Clusters Deployment and Performance Guide – Part Number B10768-02	A Services Deployment Example
Oracle® Real Application Clusters Administrator's Guide – Part Number B10765-02	Server Control (SRVCTL) Reference

Glossary

This brief glossary will help to clarify some of the terms used in this book.

Automatic Storage Management (ASM) – ASM is a 10g disk storage system created to balance the I/O of databases across multiple disk volumes. It requires the +ASM instance to be running in order to start a database instance. The 10g release 1 version of ASM has no formal file system; directories and file names are managed through database views and the +ASM instance.

Cache Fusion – When most people think of fusion, they think of a nuclear reaction that releases energy. That fantastic concept makes for a great marketing ploy; fusion just sounds cool. Oracle is using a different meaning of fusion for this term. What Oracle means by fusion is the merging of different elements. The cache is the physical memory of a node. Oracle software passes buffers from one node to another over the internal network. This keeps a consistent image of the buffer cache across all instances in the cluster, effectively fusing the caches of all instances into one unit.

Cluster or Real Application Cluster – A collection of two or more nodes that share a common external storage, a common network interconnect and use the same operating system. The nodes are configured to increase scalability and fault tolerance for an application such as an Oracle database.

Cluster Ready Services – The 10g collection of software, namely crsd, cssd, and evmd used to manage Oracle Clusters.

Cluster Ready Services Daemon (crsd) – This 10g process is run as root. It maintains database configuration information in the CRS repository file.

Cluster Synchronization Services Daemon (ocssd or cssd) -This daemon is the 10g version of what was known as "Cluster Manager" from 9i. It is a critical process for keeping the nodes synchronized.

Event Manager Daemon (evmd) – A process that is part of the 10g Cluster Ready Services. This process runs as oracle. It starts other processes (racgevt and evmlogger) to manage callouts. This daemon is configured from the file /etc/evmdaemon.conf.

Global Services Daemon (gsd) – This daemon supports srvctl, dbca and em to process requests such as database startup and shutdown.

Instance – The active part of a database is the instance. A database instance is made up of the System Global Area and the background processes. When a shutdown occurs, the database still exists as files on disk, but the instance is gone until it is started up again.

Oracle Cluster File System (ocfs) – A file system especially created to support cluster databases.

Oracle Cluster Manager Daemon (ocmd) – This 9i daemon helps to keep the nodes synchronized within the cluster.

Oracle Notification Service (ons) – This service polls the instances of the cluster to determine which is least busy, and continuously reports this information to the listeners and middle-tier connection pools. Incoming connections are passed to individual servers or dispatchers accordingly. In 9i, this functionality is accomplished by means of the PMON process, which is unable to report server usage as continuously as ONS.

Virtual IP (vip) – An IP address that can be maintained by any node in the cluster so if a node is not running, the cluster software will reassign the VIP to another node, maintaining the availability of the service (ie. listener) that it supports.

Voting Disk/Voting File – The file used to keep nodes in sync and to detect and resolve "split-brain"; a condition that occurs when the nodes in a cluster lose communication with each other and become confused about which nodes are members of the cluster and which nodes are not.

Index

About the Author

Edward Stoever is the Senior Oracle Database Administrator for Fuller Theological Seminary in Pasadena, California. His first exposure to Oracle came in 1999, when he created "Grannymail.com", one of the Internet's first sites offering real postal letters and greeting cards sent from a user's browser.

Typical to early internet ventures, Grannymail.com vanished from the web in 2002. Shortly after, Edward became an Oracle Certified Professional, both as a Database Administrator and as an Application Developer. After achieving his certifications, the technical school where Edward trained for his certification hired him as a teacher. As a student and teacher, Edward learned the importance of writing technical instructions that are concise and easily understood.

In 2003, Edward joined the Management Information Services Department at Fuller Seminary. He was quickly promoted to Senior Database Administrator. Edward is a single-father of two daughters, Scarlett and Veronica.

Shroff / Rampant TechPress

PUBLISHED TITLES

ISBN	Title	Author	Price
8173669112	Conducting the J2EE Job Interview: IT Manager Guide for J2EE with Interview Questions, *244 Pages*	Hunter	250.00
8173669147	Conducting the Java Job Interview: IT Manager Guide for Java with Interview Questions, *308 Pages*	Hunter	300.00
8173669155	Conducting the Network Administrator Job Interview: IT Manager Guide with Cisco CCNA Job Interview Questions, *146 Pages*	Haeder	150.00
8173667764	Conducting the Oracle Job Interview Tips - IT Manager Guide for Oracle Job Interviews with Interview Questions (Includes Oracle 9i), *144 Pages*	Ault	150.00
8173669139	Conducting the Programmer Job Interview: IT Manager Guide with Java, J2EE, C, C++, Unix, PHP and Oracle Interview Questions!, *308 Pages*	Burleson	300.00
8173669074	Conducting the UNIX Job Interview: IT Manager Guide with Unix Interview Questions, *180 Pages*	Haeder	200.00
8173667829	Conducting the Web Designer Job Interview: IT Manager J2EE Job Interview Questions, *308 Pages*	Burleson	300.00
8173669082	Conducting the Web Master Job Interview: IT Manager Guide with Webmaster Interview Questions!, *372 Pages*	Burleson	350.00
817366773X	Creating a Self-Tuning Oracle Database - Automating Oracle9i Dynamic SGA Performance, *156 Pages*	Burleson	150.00
8184043449	**Database Benchmarking: Practical methods for Oracle & SQL Server 2005, 211 Pages**	**Dr.Scalzo**	**225.00**
8173664927	Easy Oracle Automation: Oracle10g Automatic Storage, Memory and Diagnostic Features, *300 Pages*	Dr. Kumar	300.00
8184041152	**Easy Oracle HTML - DB : Create Dynamic Web Pages with Oracle, *400 Pages***	**Cunningham**	**375.00**
8184043295	**Easy Linux Commands: Working Examples of Linux Command Syntax, *193 Pages***	**Clark**	**225.00**
8184043287	**Easy Oracle Jumpstart: Oracle Database Management Concepts &Administration (Includes Oracle10g), *223 Pages***	**Freeman**	**250.00**
8184040466	**Easy Oracle PL/SQL Programming: Get Started Fast with Working PL/SQL Code Examples (Includes 10g), *200 Pages***	**Col. Garmany**	**150.00**
8173669813	Easy Oracle SQL: Get Started Fast Writing SQL Reports with SQL*Plus (Includes Oracle10g), *200 Pages*	Col. Garmany	225.00
8184043465	**High Performance SQL Server DBA Tuning & Optimization Secrets (Splash "SQL Server 2005 Yukon"), *305 Pages***	**Schumacher**	**325.00**
8173667810	Mike Ault's Oracle Internals Monitoring & Tuning Scripts - Advanced Internals & OCP Certification Insights for the Master DBA (Includes Oracle 10g), *368 Pages*	Ault	350.00

ISBN	Title	Author	Price
8173668523	OCP Instructor's Guide for Oracle DBA Certification: A Study Guide to Advanced Oracle Certified Professional Database Administration Techniques, *340 Pages*	Foot	325.00
817366854X	Oracle10g Grid & Real Application Clusters: Oracle10g Grid Computing with RAC, *868 Pages*	Ault	600.00
8173668558	Oracle Database 10g New Features: Oracle10g Reference for Advanced Tuning & Administration, *548 Pages*	Ault	450.00
8173664919	Oracle Dataguard: Standby Database Failover Handbook, *364 Pgs*	Kumar	325.00
8173669104	Oracle Disk I / O Tuning: Disk IO Performance & Optimization for Oracle 10g Database, *244 Pages*	Ault	250.00
8173669821	Oracle Job Scheduling: Creating Robust Task Management with dbms_job and Oracle 10g dbms_Scheduler, *288 Pages*	Dr. Hall	300.00
8173667748	Oracle Performance Troubleshooting – with Dictionary Internals SQL & Tuning Scripts (Includes Oracle 9i), *268 Pages*	Schumacher	250.00
8184043430	**Oracle PL/SQL Tuning: Expert Secrets for High Performance Programming (Includes Oracle10g), *319 Pages***	**Dr. Hall**	**300.00**
8173668515	Oracle Privacy Security Auditing: Includes Federal Law Compliance with HIPAA, Sarbanes-Oxley & The Gramm-Leach-Bliley Act GLB (Includes Oracle 10g), *692 Pages*	Nanda	575.00
8173667756	Oracle9i RAC - Oracle Real Application Clusters Configuration and Internals, *628 Pages*	Ault	500.00
8173669910	**Oracle RAC & Grid Tuning with Solid State Disk: Experts Secrets for High Performance Clustered Grid Computing (Includes Oracle10g), *208 Pages***	**Ault**	**225.00**
8173667780	Oracle Replication - Snapshot, Multi-Master & Materialized Views Scripts (Includes Oracle 10g), *244 Pages*	Garmany	250.00
8173669538	Oracle Silver Bullets: Real - World Oracle Performance Secrets, *280 Pages*	Burleson	250.00
8173669546	Oracle Solid State Disk Tuning: High Performance Oracle Tuning with RAM Disk, *204 Pages*	Burleson	200.00
8173669090	Oracle SQL Tuning & CBO Internals (Includes Oracle 10g), *354 Pgs*	Floss	350.00
8173664994	Oracle Streams: High Speed Replication & Data Sharing, *308 Pgs*	Tumma	300.00
8184041004	**Oracle Tuning: The Definitive Reference, *900 Pages***	**Danchenkov**	**600.00**
817366661X	Oracle Tuning Power Scripts with 100+ High Performance SQL Scripts, *300 Pages*	Ault	350.00
8173667772	Oracle Utilities - Using Hidden Programs, Import / Export, SQL*Loader, Oradebug, Dbverify, Tkprof & More (Includes Oracle 9i), *276 Pages*	Moore	250.00
8173664978	Oracle Wait Event Tuning: High Performance with Wait Event Interface Analysis (Includes 10g), *276 Pages*	Andert	275.00
8184043457	**Personal Oracle RAC Clusters: Create Oracle 10g Grid Computing At - Home, *292 Pages***	**Stoever**	**300.00**
8173669120	Top Answers to Job Interview Questions: Includes questions you must ask at every interview, *148 Pages*	Burleson	150.00

FORTHCOMING TITLES

June 2007

ISBN	Title	Author	Price
8184043562	Conducting the Web Services Job Interview: IT Manager Guide for Web Services Job Interviews with Delphi, .Net, XML UDDI, SOAP, ASP .NET & WSL Web Services Job Interview Questions, *256 Pages*	Brown	250.00

ISBN	Title	Author	Price
8184043570	Conducting the Windows Advanced Server Job Interview: IT Manager Guide to Windows Advanced Server Job Interviews with Itanium, .NET & Windows Advanced Server Oracle Job Interview Questions, *276 Pages*	Burleson	275.00
8184043589	Easy HTML-DB Oracle Application Express Create Dynamic Web Pages with OAE, *400 Pages*	Cunningham	375.00
8184043619	Super SQL Server Systems: Turbocharge Database Performance with C++ External Procedures, *550 Pages*	Gama	400.00
8184043627	You're Fired! Firing Computer Professionals: The IT Manager Guide for Terminating "With Cause", *240 Pages*	Papaj	250.00

August 2007

ISBN	Title	Author	Price
8184043651	Easy Oracle PHP Create Dynamic Web Pages with Oracle Data, *230 Pages*	Gogala	425.00
818404366X	High Performance SQL Server Data Warehousing Expert Data Warehouse Design and Development (SQL Server 2005), *290 Pages*	Afyouni	300.00

September 2007

ISBN	Title	Author	Price
8184043694	Easy Oracle Scalability: Practical Examples Practical for a Growing Database, *225 Pages*	Karam	250.00
8184043708	EnterpriseDB : The Definitive Reference, The Oracle - Compatible Enterprise database, *550 Pages*	Cunningham	575.00
8184043716	SQL Design Patterns: The Expert Guide to SQL Programming, *264 Pages*	Tropashko	300.00
8184043724	Oracle Best Practices Practical Standards for Success, *227 Pages*	Crotty	250.00
8184043732	Oracle Data Mining Mining Gold from your Warehouse, 300 Pages	Dr. Hamm	325.00

- Dates & Prices of forthcoming titles are tentative and subject to change without notice.
- All Prices are in Indian Rupees.
- TITLES RELEASED AFTER January 2006 ARE MARKED IN BOLD.